TEACHER INTERRUPTED

My Journey Through

Challenge Toward Courage

One Lesson, One Life,

One Student at a Time

Christy Wilson

Dear Reader Friends-- I wrote about these students and what they taught me because certain lessons were meant to be shared. My hope is that other teachers, school leaders, educators, decision makers, policy makers and students will be inspired by the stories in this book. Some are heartbreaking, but hopefully, to paraphrase Parker Palmer, they will break our hearts wide open and urge us to stand in the tragic gap between what is and what can be.

-Christy Wilson

"The most challenging students teach us the most important lessons."

"We know true equity builds community and wasted potential is tragic. Through these compelling stories about her difficult work with challenging yet beloved students, Christy has shown us why hope is essential and how we can love despite the systematic limits we face."

-Cristina Tomkins—Student Success Coach

TEACHER INTERRUPTED

My Journey Through

Challenge Toward Courage

One Lesson, One Life,

One Student at a Time

Christy Wilson

Table of Contents

Introduction   1

Chapter 1: Katy and Jesús—*What If…*   9

Chapter 2: Daniel and Danny—*Contractors, Cotillion, Blue Eyes Smiling* 21

Chapter 3: Sandy—*Architects and Fishing Rods*   45

Chapter 4: DJ—*Legos and Life*   55

Chapter 5: José—*Hate, Hurt, and Hope*   67

Chapter 6: Diego—*Gangster Dreams*   97

Chapter 7: *Dear Christian…*   121

Chapter 8: David—*Apathy and Angst*   135

Chapter 9: Grant—*Seven Words*   149

Chapter 10: Vanessa—*A Lesson in Equity*   155

Chapter 11: Ric (no K)—*Seeking Honor*   161

Chapter 12: Pablo—*Truancy and Truth*   169

Chapter 13: *Sharing Steve*   173

Chapter 14: Sabine—*Unexpected Encounter*   181

Chapter 15: Hope *(An Attempt at Concluding)*   191

Afterword   203

Acknowledgments   205

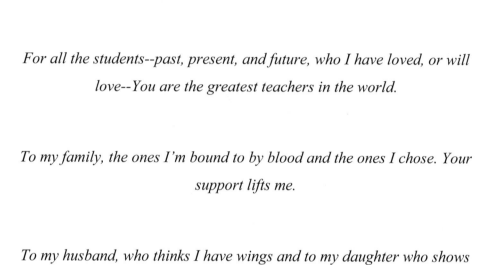

For all the students--past, present, and future, who I have loved, or will love--You are the greatest teachers in the world.

To my family, the ones I'm bound to by blood and the ones I chose. Your support lifts me.

To my husband, who thinks I have wings and to my daughter who shows me how to fly.

"The function of education is to teach one to think intensively and to think critically. Intelligence plus character - that is the goal of true education."

- Dr. Martin Luther King Jr.

"In the end, the challenge faced by adherents of every tradition of faith or reason is the same one we face in our public lives: to let the stranger—and things we find strange—be who and what they are, allowing them to open us to the vexing and enlivening mysteries we find within and around us."

- Parker Palmer

Introduction

When I was applying to colleges in 1989, I saw the movie, *Stand and Deliver*, the story of Jaime Escalante, a teacher who held out hope for a group of overlooked Latino youth. He took kids, who were years below grade level, and turned them into honors and advanced placement students. The results of his efforts were so remarkable that the testing administrators thought the students cheated and insisted they retake the exam, with increased supervision. The second results were even more remarkable. I was sold.

The idea of spending my life empowering young lives came without prelude or explanation. But it was exhilarating. And so, I set off to change the world, or at the very least, finish college and get a paying job as a teacher.

The title of this book came to me in a similar way. I wouldn't have found it had I not heard an interview with Linda Sue Park, the author of *Long Walk to Water*. She spoke about the process behind her own book's title. She described the trials of the lost boys of Sudan as well as a young girl's perilous work of walking miles to gather gallons of dirty water. While describing their plight, her mind made a subconscious connection to Nelson Mandela's story, *A Long Walk to Freedom*.

Such beautiful collisions of thought are born quietly and softly and sometimes unbeknownst to us. When I heard Linda Sue Park tell the story of her book's title, it led me to rethink my own story.

There are students in every school and classroom that interrupt the flow of instruction. They induce moments of exasperation and distraction, which interrupt concentration. A classroom teacher, who has worked thoughtfully to link instructional themes, silently screams, *"You are wasting our time!"*

And so, the title formed in my head, subconsciously linked to another story about a troubled teen, who was sent to a psychiatric hospital, where she spent two tumultuous years. Her story was brought to life through Susanna Kaysen's book, *Girl Interrupted.*

Where does sane end and insane begin? Perhaps the line is fuzzier than we care to think. Could the same be true for behavioral problems in our schools? Some feel intentional and obvious, but others are more complicated when we peel back the layers to uncover the core. Either way, classrooms are impacted and students are affected. Teachers are frustrated because everyone's education is interrupted.

In an interview, Linda Sue Park described writing as a way of exploring an idea. *"I don't write because I have all the answers, I write because I have questions."* She says readers so often teach the writer about her work.

This makes me feel a little better about writing a book that left me with more questions than answers. My hope is that we can learn from one another so that the future of education will involve more educators and more students exchanging roles, sharing their stories, and seeking to find common ground.

During my young adult life, there was a VH1 series called, *The Story Behind the Music.* It was a creative portrayal of various musicians and band members, which documented their rise from rags to riches, from obscurity to fame, from no one to someone.

Their sagas sucked me in and it became my guilty pleasure to watch a series of long episodes about even obscure artists. After 46 minutes, I was their biggest fan. Each story would unfold into an informational tale of a humble human, with a hope and a dream. I'd find myself wondering what makes one band member die of a drug overdose while others rise to the highest pinnacle of success? Why would Shania Twain overcome the shadows of doubt and poverty to become an international success while Kurt Cobain would decide life was not worth living and end it all with a shot to the head?

Two decades later, I ask the same questions about my students. I wonder how much we, their educators, contribute to their fate. It is impossible to quantify our influence, but if we could, we'd be amazed.

I often wonder about the feelings that linger in the hearts of students after we work through disciplinary issues. *What effect did my words and demeanor have?*

Did I make them want to try harder, be braver, act kinder, or did they leave feeling slighted, patronized, or misunderstood? Did they come to us like this, lost and broken, or did our system create them? What is their story? How might we contribute to a better ending?

My own journey has led me beyond shame, blame and deficit-based thinking. The more I ask and listen, the further I am moved. Student input has made me change my lesson plans and texts. Sometimes it made me cry. I often wonder about the crossing of our paths and our place in each other's lives.

Why do some come as customers and others as adversaries?

When they're not at grade level and we have to pause our instruction to address their deficits, do we consider why those deficits exist?

Whose voice do they hear in their heads and what language does it speak?

Once we consider the factors, do we disengage or find a way? We educators are miners, are we not? We find hidden treasures.

This book is about how I learned to dig…and discover true treasure. It is not about strategies or excuses, and it is not about guilt. For me, there was no "ah-ha" moment when I discovered my ability to empower students to find their strengths and tell their stories. More often than not, I found ways to connect our lessons to their lives because my first attempts failed, and I hate failing. I kept at it, faking it until I found a way of making it.

Sometimes it takes longer than I want and it is entirely inconvenient. But I dig on. Sometimes I discover the conversations I have with students are more important than the lessons I plan. *Perhaps the conversation* is *the lesson.*

Can we not stop the madness of our educational institution long enough to serve the student for whom it was intended?

Most of us went into education because we believed we could make a positive difference in our students' lives. Then we met our students and everything changed. We discovered exactly how scary and complicated it is to "stand and deliver." We found out how challenging it is to plan instruction, meet diverse academic needs, and address behavioral challenges. We came face to face with abundant energy, apathy and disillusionment. Our aspirations began to fade into despair.

But we are a brave lot, so we press on with our scary, complicated work. We find creative ways to coerce them. We tell them they're going to be okay. When it seems they won't be okay, we hold out hope anyway, like a buoy for the drowning. We don't lie to them and we don't lecture them; instead, we cast out lifelines and do the work to pull them in.

We educators stand on the front lines, regularly asking ourselves, *If not me, then who?* We do not know where such a question will take us, but we know it must be asked. We wonder, *Who better than us, and what better time than now?* And so, we summon courage. We rise, we teach, and we believe our work will render a positive impact.

Every educator's story involves discouragement, yet we dig through stubborn dirt to find lost treasures. At various points, we lose our way and forget what led us here in the first place. Our courage falters and our ability to believe in potential weakens. We're not sure how to reach challenging students in impossibly difficult circumstances. But we keep coming back because we haven't given up yet. We haven't stopped hoping. Somehow, we still believe we can stand and deliver.

I desperately wish this book could guarantee results. I wish it could map out 10 simple steps to enhanced classroom management and increased engagement. But that was not my reality. My journey with these young people was a messy and winding path. I had to let go of pride, alter my aspirations and learn to listen. I leaned into their stories, realizing I had a role in their unfolding.

Our toughest, most challenging students may teach us more about ourselves and about life than we thought possible. They will wear us down and burn us out, but if we do not give up on them or on ourselves, we will find that our labors are never in vain. After all, sowing seeds is a sweaty and complicated process. And we must stay patient while we wait for the harvest.

Beneath every educator's story is another story—the *student's* version. The work of a teacher is to learn *their* story.

In order to learn, we ask open-ended questions and listen to the honest answers that follow. We hear our students tell their stories and we tell ours. The stories are profound and tragic, beautiful and unique. They break our hearts wide open. We cannot save them, but we can inspire them.

Long ago, I discovered I was no Jaime Escalante, at least not Hollywood's version. Still, I have this story to tell, about finding common ground to stand on and a worthwhile message to deliver. I believe in some way I was destined to be their teacher, and they were destined to be mine.

I naïvely set out to be a hero, but along the way, I made a crucial discovery: Kids don't want a hero. They want someone who sits beside them long enough to listen to their harsh words and their harsh lives. Underneath their dirt is a treasure. An unforgettable story.

Sometimes the harshest stories have the worthiest lessons.

"Out beyond ideas of wrongdoing and rightdoing, there is a field. I'll meet you there."

–Rumi

Chapter 1

Katy and Jesús—*What If...*

"If the teacher believes students can succeed, she tends to behave in ways that help them succeed."

—Robert J. Marzano

About 10 years ago, Robert Marzano's work became all the rage in my district. I recall sitting in a large circle in our school library, with a group of colleagues, discussing his book, *The Art and Science of Teaching,* chapter by chapter. I read most of the book, skimmed and scanned the rest, and stopped in my tracks when I got to chapter nine.

For a short while, I struggled to put my finger on why I felt the jolt, the knot, and the conviction. After all, it was not entirely earth-shattering information. It was about holding high expectations for *all* students. I looked around our room, full of dedicated educators and thought, *"Of course, we hold high expectations for all students. We all know how important it is to do this and of course we all believe we should do this."* But I still felt the tug. I'd been struck by one particular statement and so, while the rest of the crew engaged in a lively discussion, I sat there rereading it to myself, trying to put my finger on why I felt so nudged. *"If I believed this student was completely capable of learning this content, what would I be doing right now?"*

My honest side knew exactly why this sentence gripped me, but my arrogant side decided to sit in denial and defend myself against it. My intention was to spend the remainder of the book club and evening believing it was written for "other" educators- you know, the lazy ones, who don't believe in all their students. No one I actually knew, but those "other" horrible people that give us "good teachers" a bad name.

I highlighted a few statements and continued rereading them quietly. Tuning out the voices around me, I bathed the following words in neon yellow: *"A teacher's beliefs about students' chances of success in school influence the teacher's actions with students, which in turn influence students' achievement."*

As I reread various sentences, I began to wonder about my beliefs. I knew I truly believed in most of my kids and kind-of believed (if there is such a thing) in two others. I continued highlighting and rereading: *"If the teacher believes students can succeed, she tends to behave in ways that help them succeed."*

My mind wandered off as I processed and pondered. Deep down, I knew Rob Marzano was right and I knew this chapter was meant entirely for me to read exactly now.

Still, I have a very strong ability to go deep into denial. It is a special skill-set I hold. I was not in the mood to call myself out and question my individual beliefs about my 2nd graders. That would lead to necessary change, which would take more energy and time and dedication. Until that moment, I had been fairly content, so I forged onward in attempted denial, *of course I believe in them, in all of them…don't I? I mean… I totally do…mostly…*

I continued reading, *"If…then…*

What do you mean, **IF** *Robert Marzano!!!??? I'm totally all in. I'm as dogged and dedicated as anyone-thank you very much, so you can just go on and stop talking to me about if!*

My mind was racing, *"If…then…"* but I played it cool.

When the book club ended, I went back to do some work in the classroom, but instead of working, I started obsessing, talking to myself about how much I believed in *all* my students. And even as I obsessed, two names emerged and two faces revealed themselves. The more vivid they became, the more adamant my denial.

I am not the kind of teacher to overlook a child. And even if I was, I wouldn't be able to anyway because this is the George Bush, "No Child Left Behind" era and so no one is being left behind on my watch-thank you very much (again). And while you're at it, check my test scores because they will surely prove to you that no one is being left behind. On *second thought, don't check **all** my test scores. There are two kids who have very special needs and concerns. That wouldn't be fair.*

I huffed around my classroom, straightening things up. I tried to check email, but was too distracted by the need to convince myself about how invested in my kids I was and how I was most truly believing in **ALL** my students.

On my commute home, I kept at it. *Who do I **not** believe in? No one, that's who!* My mind kept moving while the car sat still. *Dang red lights.* The light turned green. My mind spun along with my wheels, *I am not the kind of teacher to overlook a child. I'm a total believer!*

Later in the evening, while I was unloading the dishwasher, I began to question my overly confident/entirely defensive response. *Why am I so testy and edgy about a chapter from a book club discussion?* As the last bowl made its way to the cupboard, I had settled on why. I knew exactly why and I knew exactly who I was overlooking.

There, in my mind, were the faces of those two students, the ones I knew deep down and full-well that I had (secretly and unknowingly) deemed "low-expectancy." It hurt to go there because I knew that if I deemed them "low-expectancy," then I had surely been treating them as such.

This was a dismal thought, so while sorting the silverware, I jumped back into denial and continued to defend myself, like an attorney trying to recite a rebuttal for a person she knows is entirely guilty. My attorney-self spoke, *"But I don't **NOT** believe in them, I just don't think they are as capable or as bright as the others."*

Same difference. Super lame rebuttal. Stricken from the record. My judge-self asked my defense attorney-self to take a seat. And with my guard finally down, I thought a little extra about my two students. I thought about Jesús while I stir-fried the veggies and about Katy while I set the table.

But I can explain, I processed dimly, my mind talking to itself, *Jesús, well, he reads at beginning kindergarten level. His family doesn't speak English. His brother struggled in school. He's just kind of slow. That's not my fault.* My thoughts trailed off as my truthful side responded, *True, but…what if…*

Well, I continued, as I fought against my own doubts, deciding to move on to a different argument, *Katy is beyond shy. It's not my fault she doesn't participate. Every time I call on her, I have to wait two minutes for anything audible to come from her lips. Not even an elephant could be that patient. And anyway, who knows what is in her head, because it doesn't come out and when it does, her voice is so soft and muffled, you can't hear what she's saying anyway. Plus, she's ESL and she's on an IEP for speech. I mean, she has issues. Those are her issues; that's not on me. I'm doing all I can to help her find her voice. Right? Aren't I?*

I tossed and turned a little bit extra that night, struggling through my reasons and rationale, wondering about my "low expectancy" and "high expectancy" beliefs. What was I going to do about it? How would knowing this change things for me? How would it change things for Jesús and Katy?

Damn it, Robert Marzano!

The following morning on my commute to work, I turned the radio way up in an attempt to drown out my doubts.

Now what??? I thought as I pulled into our parking lot, willing my better angels to move forward with positive change.

As I settled into the classroom, nursing my cup of coffee and wounded ego, I thoughtfully considered the many ways and times I had overlooked and underserved Jesús and Katy and I made a determination. I decided to put Robert Marzano's words to the test.

What if I REALLY start to believe in Jesús and Katy as "high expectancy" students? How would I treat them if I truly thought they were superstars?

I found my Marzano book next to my computer and looked over the sentences I'd highlighted the previous evening. *What if I thought the student was completely capable…what would I be doing right now…*

And so I began my academy award-winning performance. It began as an act, an experiment of sorts, to really test myself and to test out Robert Marzano's claims. I was going to go way beyond differentiation, complimenting, and kind "teacher talk." I was going to REALLY believe in Katy and in Jesús. I was going to call on them and wait for their answers, believing they had brilliant thoughts in their brains and worthy connections on the tips of their tongues, waiting to be shared.

That very morning, I began by welcoming them more fervently and calling on them more regularly. I started hanging onto their words and nodding when they spoke. I started calling on them in the middle of discussions, telling the class things like,

"Hold onto that thought, (super high-level thinker) Makena. Before you start in, I really want to hear what Jesús thinks about this. Jesús, you always have such an interesting perspective on the characters in our stories. What do you think our protagonist is feeling?" Jesús would look at me stone-faced and shocked.

"And Katy, when he's done, I want to hear what you are predicting might happen next. You always have such thoughtful ideas, I'm going to start calling on you more so we all get a chance to hear what you are thinking." Her eyes were as wide as a doe's, staring at me as if paralyzed by the fear of an oncoming car.

Day after day, I kept at it, *"Wow Jesús, I hadn't thought of that. Your point of view is so valuable to our class. I'm going to be asking you to share a lot more from now on."* He would smile slightly. *"And Katy, your contributions to our class discussions are always so interesting. I know you are kind of shy, but I so appreciate that you are brave enough to share out loud, so we can learn from you."* She would smile timidly.

Truth be told, I was faking it. I had to push myself to remember to call on them, appear more interested, and stay patient; sometimes the "wait time" was extraordinarily long.

But after a couple of weeks, it became a habit. Pretty soon, others were asking Jesús and Katy more questions and wanting them in their groups. After a couple of months, there was no wait time. Katy and Jesús were so used to being called on regularly, they started raising their hands. It turns out, they DID have brilliant thoughts to share and connections to convey. They were not slow thinkers, they were engaged learners.

The year ended and they had both made far more than a year's worth of growth. They still lagged behind their grade level peers, but the gap was closing fast.

Since our school was a looping school, I got to keep them both as third graders. Same song, second verse. I asked them questions and oohed and aahed over their comments, their efforts, and their work. By the end of 3rd grade, Katy was thriving and Jesús was approaching grade level.

Then, when I found out that one of our 4th grade teachers was retiring, I decided to move up with this very special crew of kids. I had nine students for a third year, Jesús and Katy among them.

By then, Katy had exited out of ESL and had met all the criteria to graduate from her speech IEP. She remained introverted by nature, with a soft voice, but she was very engaged in learning and both she and Jesús passed all their benchmark tests.

I shudder to think what might have happened to both of them had I not read chapter nine of Robert Marzano's book early in their 2nd grade year. They were only seven years old and they deserved a teacher who *truly* believed in them, a teacher who didn't make excuses or explain away why they were not "on track."

The remainder of Katy's academic story is a lovely one. She was highly engaged academically and found a lovely niche of friends socially. She was peaceful and radiant to be around and was quite successful in middle and high school. I was in charge of discipline in her middle school and our paths never crossed. She had no need of discipline; she was self-disciplined, self-directed, and self-motivated. She had a quiet confidence and a gentle spirit. I had the honor of attending her high school graduation and it was entirely moving to watch her walk with grace and poise across the stage, head held high. I applauded for her a little extra, knowing she was the first person in her family to accomplish such a task.

Jesús' story is a bit more complex, but it is still noteworthy. He passed many benchmark exams, but struggled tremendously with literacy. Of all the students I taught, I remember him as my most vivid example of determination. His parents would tell me at conferences about how he would come home and teach them the things he was learning. They were a tight-knit family, who loved their son tremendously. Later, they would prove to me how far that love would take them.

One of my first and most unfortunate tasks when I began my work in handling middle school discipline was to search Jesús' locker. Jesús had fallen into a crowd that needed money. Jesús was involved with some friends in the stealing and selling of a few of his mother's prescription pills. Drugs in school being non-negotiable, Jesús was expelled and I had to sit across the table from his parents when they were told. They were heartbroken and did not want Jesús to go to the school where bad boys go, so they moved out of state for the duration of his expulsion.

Jesús and his family returned a year later and he entered our local high school. It was rough for him academically. I'd check in on him and I'd hear mixed messages about how he was doing and about who he was hanging around.

One day, I was running after work. It was dusk and there were two hooded figures walking in my direction. I pictured them to be high school boys on their way to the local park. I was half right. It was Jesús and his mom. I had not seen them since the expulsion hearing and they were soon recipients of a giant, sweaty hug. They were out, enjoying an evening walk together, arm in arm.

Jesús was in his junior year and he said school was hard. He admitted to struggling tremendously academically, but he wasn't going to give up. I reminded him that he was my definition of determination, that of all the kids I taught, when I thought about a hard worker who persevered, I would often think about him. His mom stood nodding in agreement, smiling at her beloved son. I told him not to give up, that he could do it. He nodded and smiled the familiar smile of a second grader who had become a young man. That is the last picture I have of him. He did not graduate with his class, but like all our students, his story is still being written.

Whenever I have to work with rough, off-task students who struggle with our pace and rigor, I think, *"What if..."* What if I had not been in that book club and read Rob Marzano's chapter nine? What if I had gone on believing there were just some kids who "got it" ("high-expectancy students") and others who didn't (and were never really going to—doomed to become "low expectancy students")? I cringe to consider the damage I would have caused by limiting Jesús and Katy's potential for three straight years.

That was the year I became a teacher who was going to be a believer in all her students. No more excuses. I was going to find the amazing in all of them and I was going to be overt and vocal about it, telling them regularly how much I value their perspective, the ideas they bring, the thoughts they share.

Ironically, that is also the year I became a parent. Having a child helped me internalize a parent's hopes and fears when they send their kids to school each morning. What happens if teachers deem them "low expectancy"? What happens when we *truly* believe in their abilities and potential? *What if...*

Chapter 2

Daniel and Danny—*Contractors, Cotillion, Blue Eyes Smiling*

"Don't cry because it's over. Smile because it happened."

-Dr.Seuss

As a first-year teacher, I worked at a private school in southern California. Almost all our families were well off and we were spoiled with parent involvement. I affectionately nicknamed our school "the Country Club" because there was a lot of collective wealth. All my students had the potential and the means to live out their dreams. They all had educated parents with resources and connections. I recall a student named Daniel, who was particularly sharp in math. I remember thinking he could go to Cal Tech or MIT.

One day, when I was waiting with him in the parent pick up zone, he and his best friend, Brian, were moping around, commiserating.

"What's wrong guys? It's the END of the school day; you're supposed to be free and happy."

They smiled at my joke and walked a few steps closer. *"It's Wednesday! Wednesday afternoons are the worst,"* Brian said with conviction.

"Seriously awful." added Daniel, dropping his heavy backpack on the ground beside him.

"So. What's wrong with Wednesdays?" I asked, slightly amused by their dramatic flair. They scrunched up their noses like they'd just smelled a skunk's stink hole.

"We have Cotillion on Wednesdays."

It's such a strange feeling when your students seem smarter than you. This was one of those times. I'd heard the term, but didn't really know what it was. *"Um, what's Cotillion?"*

"You are so lucky you don't know! It is this dance thing. We have to go learn to dance and learn to have good manners." They shuddered at the horrific thought.

"WITH GIRLS!" said Brian, *"It's horrible!"*

"It's the worst." added Daniel.

I almost burst out laughing! First of all, they were privileged, talented and well-versed white boys in the 3rd grade. What did they know about *"horrible"* and *"the worst"*? Secondly, they were equally adorable and hilarious trying to explain it to me. And thirdly, no wonder I didn't know what Cotillion was. I grew up poor.

I'd been raised in what Ruby Payne would call "Situational Poverty." My dad came from wealth, but had mismanaged it and lacked the discipline to live up to and/or follow through on his potential.

My mom was a hard-working farm girl, who got in over her head when she married someone with abusive and addictive tendencies. Whatever money we did have was quickly squandered.

So, my brother and I would hunt for cans and bottles before and after school to help pay for odds and ends. We cringed to ask for money for a school field trip or for new shoes. And we were notorious for wearing off brand and hand-me-down items. Cotillion was the least of our worries.

Having a background such as this felt like a curse as I worked my way through high school, but it would later serve me well. When one is comparatively poor, it is hard to feel entitled or smug. Being poor means you have to work hard for what you have and harder for what you want.

I'm not saying the rich don't work hard. I've had several hard-working millionaire friends who were incredibly generous and gracious to me. What I'm saying is that my background has helped me relate to my students, especially those who are barely scraping by, struggling to stay afloat, worried about how to pay the four-dollar fee for their holiday concert ticket.

But at this particular moment in the parent pick up zone of "the Country Club," on this fine, sunny Wednesday, there was not a lot I could contribute to our Cotillion conversation.

"Wait, how do you pronounce it again?" I asked as the boys smiled up at me, amused by my interest as well as my lack of knowledge.

"Ca-till-ee-un." they said as they made barfing sounds.

"And what is it again?" I asked, trying not to sound as ignorant as I was.

"You're better off not knowing. Mostly it's about rules and manners, but today we have to get all dressed up and dance with girls."

"Sounds like prom." I said. *"And prom was fun."*

"What's prom?" they asked, with a new look of horror, like something else, equally undesirable, or possibly even worse, might present itself when they least expected it. Doomed to a 3rd grade boy's most dreaded fate--dancing with girls.

And so, our conversation went, round and round, until their moms came to pick them up. When Daniel's mom arrived, there was something (besides Cotillion) that I'd wanted to discuss with her.

Earlier that day, when Daniel was explaining some of his mathematical thinking, and I was, as usual, in awe, I asked him what he wanted to be when he grew up. I'd envisioned him saying, "college professor" or "systems analyst" or "computer programmer," all very respectable jobs for a budding mathematician in the mid 90s. Instead, he surprised me by saying *"A contractor."*

"I'm sorry, what?" I said, thinking I'd misunderstood.

"A contractor. I want to build things and work with my hands." He explained as he lifted up his tiny, pale hands for a double high five.

"Oh. I see," I said, returning the "high ten" while trying to hide my disappointment. A private conversation inside my head continued*: Why would a bright kid like you want to be a contractor?*

The truth was, I had no idea what a contractor actually did. In my limited life, we'd had no need to hire a contractor. People who struggle to make rent typically don't hire contractors. I had no idea what responsibilities they held nor what skill sets they needed to master.

At that point in my life, I knew only one contractor. He lived up the street from me when I was young. I used to play with his daughter and one day she told me he had Playboy magazines hidden under the bed. He always looked dirty and he spit and cussed regularly. That was my one single snapshot of a contractor and Daniel didn't fit that. So, I wanted to talk with Daniel's mom about his future.

When she came up to get Daniel and to say good bye, I made a joking comment about Cotillion. She had a good nature to go along with her good looks and she laughed. *"I know, he hates it. But I want him to grow up to be a gentleman."*

"I get it." I said (though I really didn't get it because before five minutes ago, I didn't even know what it was. My brother didn't go to Cotillion and he seemed to be a gentleman, but whatever.)

I went on to explain about my conversation with Daniel during math and about how he wanted to be a contractor. Her expression let me know she was thinking along the same lines.

"I know. He's pretty set on that. I hope he changes his mind. I mean, he's got a lot of years left. But contractors don't have to go to college and we'd like him to go to a good school."

I nodded as I stared at her soft blond hair that glowed with the sun behind it. I complimented her beautiful dress and shoes and off she went, with Daniel waving good-bye, smiling and saying something funny about why couldn't he just stay longer and miss Cotillion.

These little snippets come back to me, a lifetime of conversations with hundreds of students and their family members, like flashback scenes from a TV comedy rerun, where I cringe because the protagonist does something so foolish it becomes comical. Only this time, I am not laughing because I am looking at myself from the outside in and I am seeing a teacher judge a dream. She had the chance to foster it and fuel it, but instead, she doubted it.

A quarter of a century later, that memory of Cotillion Wednesday is a freeze frame around a faulty notion I constructed, informed only by my own upbringing and limited by the isolation of my own thoughts about what a "good job" was. I made and shared assumptions that talented and successful people should all go to "good colleges" and do "good things" and stay on a "good career path," whatever that might mean.

I made a judgement about Daniel's dream and took time to talk with his mom about my concerns about this dream. And as I write these words, I'm thinking, *"Who am I to squash a 3rd grade boy's dream? What makes me the dream keeper?"*

The sweet, bright kid wanted to work with his hands and use his vast skillsets to build and create. That would be a gift to society and honest, profitable work, but there I stood, in his way, judging an 8-year old's ambition, with his mother's support.

I've since hired several contractors and I've appreciated their mathematical and engineering skills as well as their personable natures. One of them reminded me of an older version of Daniel and I cringed once again at the thought of a young teacher trying to steer a young man away from such a noble professional dream.

A few years later, when I moved away from "the Country Club" to work in the inner city, I met an unforgettable young man, also named Daniel, (only we all called him Danny). If Danny had told me he wanted to be a contractor, I'd probably have commended his choice. And why not? That's a respectable job for a brown kid from the hood with no mom and a dad who works at Denny's.

I look back with a bit of shame at my young teacher self. Who said we should save all "the good jobs," "the college jobs" for rich suburban boys with high math scores who go to Cotillion?

I didn't realize at first, just how culturally insensitive and flawed my thinking was for a lot of reasons. Sure, I had black friends and Latina friends, but I thought their lives were mostly like mine, except that they had darker skin, or spoke Spanish to their parents. As a product of my own race and privilege, I knew very little about the statistical, systematic, and historical disadvantages of others.

I hadn't met the heroes of the following chapters yet. I hadn't studied the effects of racism on education or read Nelson Mandela, Maya Angelou, Jacqueline Woodson or Jazmine Ward's books. I hadn't schooled myself on the apartheid effect, nor had I looked at the habits and traditions of education through the eyes of brown-skinned gangsters. I had a lot to learn.

***

Are you smarter than a 5th grader? Remember that show? Well, long before it surfaced, I'm pretty sure I learned that I was not. Or at least I questioned the matter.

I'd moved from the well-to-do suburbs to the inner city. My previous site, "the Country Club," was filled with motivated, high achieving students, and parents who were highly involved. I had so many parents who wanted to help, I had to put them on a rotating schedule. That idea would amuse me later as I found my niche in Title 1, high poverty schools, where parents work long and inflexible hours and/or are too preoccupied with survival needs to spend hours volunteering.

In my new school, 100% of my students were on free and reduced lunch and 100% of my students were from families who spoke Spanish as a first language. Also, 100% of my students were amazing, and I found myself regularly inspired by their courage and worldview. They were hard-working and kind-hearted. Universally, individually and collectively, I adored them.

I taught there for three years before relocating to the Northwest. But I am getting ahead of myself. First, I must describe a bit of the culture shock I experienced upon my move from riches to rags.

I had 24 hours to move into and organize a musty brown room, laden with outdated textbooks and dusty dictionaries. There was no internet then, no computers in the classroom, but there should have been at least a whiteboard. This room had nothing that was white. Everything was an inexplicable shade of brown, including the floor tiles, that had perhaps, at one point, been white.

I started unpacking and realized that neither of the chalkboards had chalk. I made a note to myself and kept working. I was sweating because it was summer and there was no air conditioning. I was also down to the wire with only a few more hours to make this musty room a learning home. Soon, 5th graders would arrive, expecting desks to sit at, books to read, and classroom supplies to use. When I could stand the dust bunnies no longer, I went in search of a broom…and some chalk.

The warm sunshine and the outdoor-layout of the one-story building made it appealing to explore. I soon ran into a rather friendly looking teacher. I smiled and introduced myself. She looked at me as if to say, *"Good luck, honey."*

We exchanged a few pleasantries and before we parted ways, I asked, *"Verna, where can I find some chalk?"* She looked at me with wise, aged eyes that hesitated to burst my enthusiastic bubble and answered, *"Well, did you bring any chalk?"*

"Um. No. I didn't think to." I said, suddenly feeling shy and insecure.

"Well baby, you come on into my room and I will hook you up. But you need to hear this, I don't know where you came from, but around here, you gotta bring your own supplies. You hear me?"

"I hear you." I felt like a student who had neglected to do her homework, disappointing her teacher.

It didn't take me long to figure out the ropes and to learn that the community was patient and willing to make do without complaining. It was amazing to me how little we had and how creative we became. I credit my students and their spirit of gratitude along with their tremendous work ethic.

One day, I went out and bought eight packs of Crayola markers. I hadn't gotten my paycheck yet, so I couldn't spring for each student to have their own, but I bought enough for the table groups of four to share. When I passed them out, the kids brightened, *"Look! New markers!"* They were smelling them and testing them and sharing them happily. Many were quick to say thank you and they went straight to work.

I smiled to myself remembering how at "the Country Club," the students had their own small suitcases, brimming with supplies. They had compasses, fancy calculators, their own set of crayons, highlighters, and a

24-pack of Crayola markers, including "skin" color, whatever that might be.

My new 5th graders were various shades of brown and they were just as pleased with the meager supplies I'd provided as my affluent students were with their extensive provisions.

The students brought me treasures in return: flowers from gardens, hand-written notes, pictures drawn, and small trinkets from the Dollar Store. They were always bringing and sharing treasures. And they would often stick around after school to help. Those were beautiful years.

But they were first embarrassing and difficult years. I had no prior experience working with second language learners and I felt ill-equipped and in desperate need of training.

I remember working with a student named Crystal on her journal, attempting to help correct some of the glaring grammatical errors. I did what had worked at "the Country Club" with my 3rd graders: *"Crystal, do we say, 'He don't got none?"*

She looked at me sweetly as if to say, *"I do, but the fact that you're asking me makes me wonder. I don't know, you are the teacher, you tell me."*

That's all I had. One strategy that worked with students from highly educated backgrounds. I needed new strategies.

Beyond my lagging skills with English as a Second Language instruction, there was a behavioral management learning curve as well. I was amazed at the volume and buzzing enthusiasm. Most of these students came from large and highly interactive families. They were chatty and energetic. And at any given time, we had between 30 and 35 students sharing a humble learning space.

My first day, the principal walked in to check on me and asked how it was going. I don't think she expected such an honest answer, but I truthfully replied, *"This group is much louder than my previous classes."* She looked at me matter-of-factly, and said something to the effect of, *"Well, you're their leader, what are you going to do about it? Don't blame the kids. Lead them. They will follow you."*

By the end of the first week, I'd had the opportunity to do some academic assessments and guess what? These 5th graders were WAY lower in basic math and reading skills than my 3rd graders at "the Country Club."

At the end of the day, I found myself explaining this to the assistant principal. She warmly shook my hand and said, *"Welcome to the inner city. Your job is to take them from where they are and move them forward."*

Her words became my mantra.

Still, there was no lesson greater than Danny Chavez. He came to me my second year. He was the only student I taught at that school who had blue eyes. They were a soft and subtle blue, almost gray, like the sky above the ocean when the marine layer begins to burn off. His eyes were as giant as he was tiny. Oh, so tiny. One might have assumed (falsely) that he was too tiny to cause problems.

The morning I met Danny, I was wandering around the room greeting students and helping them find their seats. From across the room, I heard a cocky voice, far too large to have come from such a tiny body, *"I'm not going to sit down and I'm not going to do any work."*

The room stalled. Everyone froze and looked at me wondering what their new teacher would do and say.

I paused, considering my options, searching for a productive response. A soft voice challenged the silence. It came from a well-meaning sweetheart.

"He's the bad one." she said, feeling sorry for me and I imagine for herself as well. Another year with Danny, a small, but mighty, resistant force. It was clear she was not alone in her reluctance to be associated with Danny's rebellious nature. Several other students were nodding their heads in agreement.

My heart rate increased and sweat marks made their way to my arm pits as I stood there pondering my next move. I thought about the comment I'd just heard *"He's the bad one"* and wondered how that label must have felt. What choice would someone with such a label have, other than to act badly?

I seized the moment and asked for everyone's attention, which was easy because they were already watching me, gaping with some combination of curiosity, amusement, and pity. How was the new teacher going to handle Danny Chavez?

"You know, everyone, 4th grade was a long time ago." I began, and as I was speaking, I realized how ridiculous this must have sounded because for this crew, 4th grade happened exactly one week ago. This was a year-round school and students got one week off before beginning their next school year.

I soldiered on, *"What happened last year is in the past."* I saw a few relieved faces among those who were still trying to figure out how a week ago counted as "the past."

"It doesn't matter to me who was a 'bad one' or a 'good one'. Everyone gets to be who they want to be. Everyone gets a fresh start. If Danny doesn't want to sit down, he's got his reasons, but that doesn't make him bad. He and I will figure things out. Let's move on so I can introduce myself and begin getting to know each of you."

Thankfully, the first activity was more of a game than an assignment. It required students to mill around the room writing down the names of classmates under various categories: Who has the longest hair? Who is the tallest?

Admittedly, in a school where almost every girl had long black hair and every boy was approximately the same height, the activity was rather lame as my categories clearly lacked imagination. Yet thankfully, it afforded me an opportunity to go over and chat with Danny.

I began, *"First of all, I should have a category on this sheet for the most amazing eyes. That would be you."* He looked up at me and gave an unmistakable and disarmed smile.

"Secondly, you don't have to sit down if you don't want to. But, if you get tired of standing, that's your desk over there." He nodded.

"And, because it's hard to write standing up, you can use my clipboard." He accepted the clipboard, looked at me, tentatively, as if waiting to see how I was going to address the "I'm not going to do any work" comment.

I continued, *"I don't know what happened in 4th grade. And truthfully, it's none of my business. But in 5th grade, we have to do some work. If you need help, I'll help you. In fact, I don't have any plans during recess and you and I can fill this out together. You can help me learn everyone's names."*

I didn't really know if that was the right thing to say. I couldn't think what else I should say, but I got lucky. Danny left me standing there, mid-thought and disappeared to join his classmates in the activity.

I later learned the reason for the accidental magic that had transpired. Danny Chavez lived for recess. The very LAST thing he wanted to do during recess was sit and do a stupid game sheet with his new teacher.

As I watched Danny mill around with his clipboard, talking to classmates and putting down names into appropriate categories, I smiled because he amused me. He looked up and saw me.

As he turned away to avoid my gaze, I realized that I liked him already. He was going to be a new kind of challenge. He was going to give me a run for my money. He was one of a kind. And I had no idea how to teach him.

There was a second activity to follow the first and I noticed Danny begin to inch toward his seat. He moved as if he was entering a cold swimming pool, one toe at a time. Slinking toward his faux wooden desk, drawing as little attention to himself as possible.

I pretended to ignore him, but when I snuck glances in his direction, he appeared to be doing exactly what he was supposed to be doing. I was careful not to call attention to it because in moments like these, 5th graders don't want to admit defeat. Saving face is paramount.

Soon enough, it was time for recess. Danny waited eagerly in line. Shifting quickly from one foot to the other, fidgeting, smiling, eager, like a race horse at the gate. He made sure I knew his paper was on my desk so he would NOT have to stay in. When I walked the class out, I asked Danny to stay behind, just long enough to let him know I was impressed with how quickly he was figuring out how to handle himself in 5th grade. He smiled and nodded and ran off to play.

The day ended for the kids, but I had to stay late to work. It was only day one and I was already worried about how I was going to meet the diverse and complex needs in the classroom. And what the hell was I going to do about Danny?

When I left, I was careful to lock my classroom door as I'd been instructed. Theft was an issue. The lock was rusty and jammed, which gave me extra time to stare at the door and wonder who was in charge of choosing the rusty burnt brick-red paint, so chipped and faded from the

California sun. I wondered why these kids didn't deserve modern colors and fresh paint?

It was dusk in "the hood," so I approached the parking lot with caution. There were no other cars and no signs of life. Then a dark figure emerged, circling. It took me a moment to realize it was a kid on a bike. It was Danny. He was riding in circles around the parking lot. As if waiting for me. But not. *Why would he be waiting for me?* As I approached my car, he rode further away.

He yelled, *"Good night Ms. Wilson."*

I looked up. He rode under a street lamp and I could see him smiling at me.

"Good night, Danny. See you tomorrow." He waved with one hand and rode off, disappearing into the darkness.

There are these moments, and with them come notions, that pass through the minds of teachers around the globe, *"How am I going to get through this?" "Do I have what it takes to rise to this challenge?" "What am I doing?" "What am I going to do next?" "What have I not yet tried?" "How soon can I retire?"* I was 25 years old and these age-old questions spun their webs to tangle my thoughts.

I had no idea what I was going to do with Danny. I drove home thinking about him, wondering how I was going to reach him, let alone teach him and get him to do any work without threatening or bribing him.

The next morning, I unlocked my classroom door and there was a note sitting on my desk. I never did learn how it made its way through a locked door and the mystery of it amused me.

> ***Dr***
>
> ***Ms Wlson***
>
> ***Tanks fr no***
>
> ***yelin a mi.***
>
> ***Danny***

The note resembled something a 5-year-old might write. No wonder Danny did not want to sit down or do any work. He was embarrassed to show his new teacher exactly what his work would look like. He knew he could not spell or write or hold a pencil the way a 5th grader was supposed to, so he figured out a plan B. Resist and rebel.

When the kids arrived, I winked at Danny and nodded in the direction of the note. He smiled and nodded back. Any time I saw him attempting work, I praised his effort and his creativity. It didn't solve the struggle because he wasn't into anything that involved books or paper. He was, however, all about the clock.

He watched it the way a dog looks at his toy under the couch, out of reach, willing it to move closer. Every now and then, Danny would shout out live time updates as recess approached, *"22 minutes till recess...14 minutes till recess...9 minutes till recess!"*

"Geez, this is going to be a long year!" I thought, but bit my tongue to keep from saying it aloud. I checked my eyes to make sure they weren't rolling.

"Um, Danny. I have an idea. I see you are really good at telling time. How about if you give me a signal, five minutes before recess, just to make sure I bring closure to our lesson on time?"

Danny smiled. *"How about if I raise my hand?"*

"Perfect." I said. *"If you shout out, it might distract me and then, if I lose my train of thought, the lesson might take longer and that would waste our recess time."*

"Done. I won't shout out." Again, he smiled. He looked around triumphantly as if he'd been awarded a distinguished honor.

In time, he raised his hand for other things. I took note of his keen interest in Low Rider cars. Looking for ways to connect with him, I began asking him more about them. He would light up like a firefly. Smiling as he talked in great detail about car colors and parts I'd never bothered to learn. When I didn't know what something was, he'd draw a diagram for me and explain it. That gave me an idea.

"Danny, you know how you hate writing and do everything you can to avoid it."

He smiled, *"Yeah."*

"What if you wrote about Low Rider cars?"

His eyebrows lifted, *"Can I draw pictures too?"*

"Of course. But you have to really write, I mean explain things with your pencil the way you do when we talk."

"Ok." He said, not bothering to suppress his emerging smile.

And that was the first day I saw him write without verbal prompting and incessant reminders.

That afternoon, he lingered behind after everyone else left. *"Ms. Wilson, can I bring in some of my Low Rider magazines to help with my writing?"*

"Um." I hesitated, then added, *"As long as they are appropriate for school."*

"Right. I will rip out some of the ads tonight. Thanks." And he whizzed off like an arrow toward a target.

And so, it began. Danny invested himself in his writing and by default, his reading too. After a few weeks, he asked if he could sit in the

"Author's Chair." He wanted to read his story to the class. At some point, I stopped cringing at all of the grammatical errors and lost myself in his smile and his enthusiasm for sharing his writing.

The months marched forward and I noted three had passed since Danny announced he wouldn't sit down and he wouldn't do any work. That former kid was long gone. It was time for a new goal.

A few weeks before our Parent-Teacher conferences, I started a private effort to involve Danny's dad in his education. Rumor was, there was no mom in the picture and Danny's dad hadn't come to any conferences or school events. Ever.

Every day, every hour, I'd watch Danny with the intent to find something special that I could comment on. And so began my shameless manipulation.

"Wow, Danny, what a creative sentence... I can't wait to share with your dad at conferences about the motivated author you've become"... "Danny, your math skills are really improving. I can't wait to tell your dad about how well you're grasping important concepts"... "These are really impressive sketches. When your dad comes to conferences, I'm going to show him how talented you are."

And so on and so forth. Shameless? Yes. Manipulative? Perhaps. Effective? Definitely. Three weeks later Danny and his dad walked through the door.

The other thing that came through the door was an unmistakable waft of onion odor. His dad was a chef at Denny's and had clearly come straight from work, stained apron and all. His expression told me he was exhausted and would rather be anywhere else on the planet BESIDES his son's classroom, but Danny had literally dragged him. I shook his hand wildly and was beyond animated as I gushed to showcase Danny's strengths. Danny sat beside me beaming.

I have taught hundreds of kids and I'm unable to remember all of their names. Without a picture, I wouldn't remember many faces. But Danny's smile is etched in my mind. I remember him sitting next to his dad. I still see his profile and the way his thin dusty hair parted to the side. I remember looking at his exhausted father, with jet black hair and deep grooves on his dark face. His demeanor told the story of a life with too many hardships and too little joy. His deep chocolate skin contrasted Danny's light olive tone. I wondered where Danny got his blue eyes and soft features. I wondered about his mom.

Five months later, I would get a little choked up to say good-bye to him as he set forth for middle school. That year, I was the closest thing he had to a mother.

Sometimes I wonder about how it all could have been different. What if I had yelled at Danny, or threatened him, or told him he had to sit down and he had to do work, or else…? What if he wasn't so prone to smiling at me when I gave him even the slightest benefit of the doubt? What if I hadn't found a way to connect with him over Low Rider cars?

He's the kind of kid that reminds me that I'm not always smarter than a 5th grader. Sometimes, I don't know what I'm doing and I don't know if what I'm doing will work, but I keep at it, looking for a way in, a connection. Danny taught me that showing up and trying my best every day is worth it. It meant something to him that I asked about his world and his interests.

Somewhere in this wide world, Danny is an adult, about the age I was when I was his teacher. Maybe he even remembers reading his story about Low Riders to our class. Maybe he designs them now. Maybe he works on them. Maybe he teaches university or performs surgery. Maybe he works as a chef like his dad. Wherever he is, I hope his joys outnumber his hardships. I hope his blue eyes are still smiling.

Chapter 3

Sandy—*Architects and Fishing Rods*

"There's no way to know what makes one thing happen and not another.
What leads to what. What destroys what. What causes what to flourish
or die or take another course."

-Cheryl Strayed, *Wild*

I've spent my adult life teaching geniuses and struggling students and young people with crazy, insane work ethics. To this day, I remain inspired by a soft-spoken 5th grader named Sandy Silva, for being all of the above.

Sandy was one of those students a teacher can count on, the one she writes down in her sub plans, *"If you don't know where it is…or what to do…or where to go…or when…just ask Sandy Silva."* Sandy was a hard-working go-getter with a soft voice and gentle spirit. She was almost as tall as me, 5'5'' with work shoes on. She was round-faced, with mocha skin and curly hair. Her hair was so thick and curly that I bet if she'd brushed it out, it would have been as tall and wide as it was long, but she always wore it in a sensible braid. Sandy did everything sensibly.

Everyone liked her, the teachers, the boys, the girls, the little siblings, everyone. She was impossible not to like. She was honest too.

I remember when I asked the kids to write a journal entry about their favorite teacher, everyone wrote about me (smart move on their part because they knew a boosted ego could possibly mean a boosted grade). But not Sandy. She wrote about her 3rd grade teacher and had the kindness to write a note of apology to me that it wasn't me. It probably went something like this:

"My favorite teacher is Ms. Ochoa—Sorry Ms. Wilson, but she was. She has a wonderful sense of humor—you do too Ms. Wilson, but she is funnier. Ms. Ochoa is so prepared for her lessons and I learned so much from her—No offense Ms. Wilson because I know you are trying your best…" and so on…

One day, when I was struck by amazement at Sandy for the thousandth time, I asked her what she wanted to be when she grew up. She said she wanted to be an architect. Her response caught me off guard because it was the kind of thing one of the kids in "the Country Club" might have said, but this was the inner city. How did Sandy Silva know what an architect did? I wondered if her dad built houses, so I asked,

"What does your dad do for work, Sandy?"

She replied nonchalantly, *"He clips yards. Why?"*

"Um." I couldn't say my real answer, which was based on my then, quite limited, view of the world. My real answer would have sounded something like, *"Because I didn't even know what an architect was when I was a 5th grader and you want to be one. That is especially amazing to me because you live in the middle of a city that is kind of known for being poor and to say, as a Latina female in 1998 that you want to be an architect is something that I, with my limited white-person perspective, think is amazing."*

Instead of saying that, I responded, *"No reason. What does your mom do?"*

Perhaps this would lead me to understand how Sandy had come upon such a dream.

"She cleans houses. Why?"

"Oh, I was just wondering. I was curious about how you know about architects and I wondered if maybe your mom or dad had a job that was connected to that career." I said, trying to sound less biased and ignorant than I was.

Sandy did not seem slighted and did not skip a beat. *"No. I just read about what they do and I think it's amazing how they can design and create beautiful homes and offices and buildings."*

The thing about Sandy is that she had this drive to work hard and to know more. She never felt stifled or limited or entitled. I took a special liking to her, mostly because she motivated me to be a better person and teacher.

The inner-city schools were over-crowded, so we were on a year-long schedule, with various months off. During those months, another group of students would move into our classroom.

After one such stint, we were re-organizing our desks and moving things back to where they had been a month before. As we slid desks across the tile, I asked the kids who were helping me what they had done during their time off.

It always amazed me that our school was located 13 minutes from the beach and none of them ever went there on vacation. They went to the local mall, to cousins' birthday parties, to Mexico to visit family, and often, stayed around town, just roaming, playing at a park nearby or helping to baby-sit their siblings.

Sandy didn't do any of those things. She and her sister would help her mom clean houses. They would drive with her to the hills of affluency and help her work. Sandy didn't seem to mind it, or if she did, she didn't let it show. I remember asking her what all she did to help and she described every last chore I'd ever hated doing when I was growing up. This is how the amazing Sandy Silva spent her vacations:

"Well, first, I empty all the trash cans in all the rooms. There are a lot of rooms. Then, I sweep the kitchen floor. I sweep outside too. My sister

and I fold all the laundry and help put the clean sheets on all the beds. We do almost everything except vacuum. My mom has to do the vacuuming because we don't get the lines right."

"The lines right???" I asked, wondering what she meant.

"Yeah, there is a way you are supposed to vacuum so the lines show up perfect on the carpet."

Once again, my 5th grader was smarter than me. I didn't know there was such a thing. I guess that's one advantage to growing up in a home with crappy carpet; you don't have to worry about getting the lines right when you vacuum.

And so, the year marched on and Sandy and I found a lot to talk about beyond house cleaning. She drank up the information I presented and she questioned everything. The thing about her questions was they were always perfectly timed and kindly worded. They enhanced the discussion and caused others, who might otherwise have tuned out, to lean in and engage.

Sandy Silva enhanced my impact and expanded my lessons. She poured herself into learning and we were all better because of her.

At the end of the year, my kids went off to middle school and I went off to Oregon. Ironically, my husband got a job in a huge architectural firm there. Sandy would have liked knowing that and she probably would have aspired to work there had she known.

In time, I lost track of all my CA kids. Such was life before Facebook and Google. One of my students had a computer and she emailed me regularly for a while, but eventually we lost track of each other too.

Memories don't fade, but our new experiences pile up and crowd the spaces where older memories live. About a month ago, I had cause to summon my memories of Sandy Silva to the surface. I was talking to a colleague about the importance of ushering in students' dreams. I told her about my former student from the inner city who wanted to be an architect, whose mom was a maid and whose dad was a gardener, who saw no reason to limit her own potential. As I was talking, I realized that Sandy would now be old enough to be in her career. I wondered if she'd become an architect.

I started Googling her name with the word architect and the name of her home town. Within 10 minutes, I saw a Facebook picture of her soft, sweet face and unmistakable curls. She was not an architect, she was a Dr. of Physical Therapy working at a large and prestigious medical institution in Minnesota.

I called the number listed and left her a voice mail. She called back, and her respectful soft-spoken tone took me back in time. She had never been much of an athlete, but here she was helping athletes. I had been an athlete, but had not previously had a need for a physical therapist.

Now, our paths were crossing. I was on leave for a severe knee injury I'd incurred by being overly aggressive in a competitive tennis match. (Basically, my 45-year-old-self forgot I was not in college anymore.) I laid in bed wondering, among other things, how a slice of my hamstring could actually become my new ACL.

Once again, Sandy knew more than me. She talked me through my road to recovery. The time off of work gave me time to reconnect with my past, to see the fruit of my labor, or more-so, the fruit of hers. Her story is incredible and it reminds me how important it is to recognize the value of a dream and to usher it forth.

Before I go into Sandy's story, I must frame it. The best way I know to do this is to borrow words and wisdom from Trevor Noah, the witty and brilliant anchor of *The Daily Show*, a well-traveled and well-spoken comedian. He wrote a book called *Born a Crime* and in it he describes his life growing up, half-black, in South Africa during the apartheid years and the aftermath of those years. He talks about a hand out, a gift from a friend that gave him a shot, a chance, an opportunity in a world where the odds were stacked against him. He wrote,

"People always lecture the poor: 'Take responsibility for yourself! Make something of yourself!' But with what raw materials are the poor to make something of themselves? People say, 'Give a man a fish, and he'll eat for a day. Teach him to fish, and he'll eat for a lifetime.' What they don't say is, 'And it would be nice if you gave him a fishing rod.'

People say, 'Oh, that's a handout.' No. I still have to work to profit by it. But I don't stand a chance without it."

When I read his words, I thought of Sandy. Someone gave her a fishing rod, a shot, a rare opportunity. She took it. She worked hard and her labors were not without great sacrifice. But she was given a boost onto a path that led her to a college scholarship and a profitable career, an appropriate challenge and reward for a bright mind like hers.

As I suffered through bedrest, waiting for my knee to heal, Sandy emailed me, updating me on her post-5th grade life:

"The greatest opportunity for me in middle school was being selected to apply to the A Better Chance *program. It is a national organization that is dedicated to helping students of color become highly educated scholars and if necessary, helping financially with college. At first, I declined the opportunity as I did not want to leave home. Then my parents encouraged me to apply and next thing you know, I was headed to Minnesota to start high school! The program hosts many students in many elite high schools across the nation. I was chosen for a boarding school in New Hampshire and for a public school in Minnesota. I decided MN was a better fit.*

"Moving to MN at fifteen was very exciting at first, but after a few months, I realized that I would not get to see my family for many months. We only had the opportunity to fly home during Christmas and summer. I

was saddened that I had to sacrifice precious time with my family, but knew that it would one day be worth it.

"My experience in the ABC program taught me more than I could have ever imagined. I matured very quickly. I learned that hard work, determination and a fighting spirit are essential for achieving goals. My plan was to return home and attend college at San Diego to be closer to my family, but life took me in a different direction.

"While I was accepted to San Diego, I could not pass up the opportunity to attend a private college here in MN on a full scholarship. So, I decided to stay another four years as I already knew how to deal with the winters. College was great, I made such lasting friendships, really, I gained all my MN family through college. In college, I studied exercise physiology and biology which helped prepare me for graduate school.

"Graduate school was even better than college! But it was also in MN! My entire family was very supportive, by that time they knew that I had made MN my new home."

The words of this email became wavy and blurred as I blinked back my tears. They were the tears of a proud teacher, excited to discover that her bright learner was given an opportunity to rise and excel. *A Better Chance* program had given Sandy a "fishing rod." And with the fishing rod Sandy was offered, she learned to fish and help others do the same.

She is in a profitable, professional, competitive and lucrative career and she is still very young. Sounds like she became the architect of her life after all, building a family, community, and client base piece by piece.

Chapter 4

DJ—*Legos and Life*

"Hold fast to dreams
For if dreams die
Life is a broken-winged bird
That cannot fly.
Hold fast to dreams
For when dreams go
Life is a barren field
Frozen with snow."

–Langston Hughes

DJ Adams was one of those kids that you would hear about in the teacher's room and see around the school, even when you weren't his teacher, or teaching his grade. I first heard about him when he was a 1st grader and I was a 3rd grade teacher.

I would see him in and around the office and I would hear stories about the creative approaches to addressing whatever his problems seemed to be. I heard he was really good at drawing trucks, which he did whenever he was sent to his "buddy classroom" when he needed "a break" from his learning environment (or when his learning environment needed a break from him).

Every now and then, I'd see him sitting in a hallway or walking around with an administrator and he would look angry, as if, in spite of his young age, he'd already come to know the world was an unjust place. At one point, I heard our student manager tell him, *"DJ, we need you to be a 'good boy!' Can I trust you to be a 'good boy?'"* And he looked at her like that was the meanest thing anyone had ever said to him.

I heard about him when he was a 2nd grader too. I was also teaching 2nd grade that year and again, there were storm clouds of frustration that swirled around him and those who tried to work with him. My friend was his teacher. She was a newer teacher, who blamed herself for not having the right tools and strategies to help him. I'm a little fuzzy on the details of his behavior that year because I was pregnant and it is entirely possible that I was fuzzy on more than my share of details. But at some point, in my fuzzy state of existence, it was explained to me that I would be DJ's next teacher.

When DJ was a 3rd grader, they put him in my class. We had all looped up with our 2nd graders, which was a trademark of our elementary school, deemed a "looping school," with a philosophy bent toward building strong classroom communities in a high mobility setting. But DJ's family and his teacher felt it would be better for him to have a "fresh start." I did not have any notions that I could do any better with him than anyone else, but I'd been teaching longer than the others and there was a hope that my experience would create a silver bullet.

For DJ's first three months of 3rd grade, I was on maternity leave. I checked in regularly with my long-term sub to see how my kids were doing. She was the perfect match for DJ and the start of the year proved to be his best yet.

As I prepared to return, I took careful note of her suggestions and strategies. She didn't push him too hard, she gave him a lot of space and quiet support, when she sensed he was edgy, she backed off.

Whew. Good thing he started the year with her! I'm not generally inclined to back off. But DJ was one of a kind and I was going to have to widen my skill set.

That was a special year, my first as a parent. Each day, I worked to be the kind of teacher I'd want my own child to have. I thought about how precious DJ must have been as a newborn to his parents, of the incredible gift he was, the joy they found in their beloved son. I tried to get to know DJ, to understand what made him tick and found his parents to be very supportive of my efforts.

DJ loved Legos. He loved to be precise and focused in his building efforts. He did not like to write. He hated trying to form letters and resented my continual reminders about fixing his capital Ds in the middle of his words. He liked his capital Ds. He hated erasing. He also hated noise.

He would cover his ears at assemblies and rock back and forth. Fire drills stressed him out entirely. If a classmate made a loud sound or distracted him, DJ would get angry at them and sometimes yell unnecessarily, not to be mean, but to be firm. I think he felt different and this was his way of standing up for himself and his needs.

As I would work with DJ on tone of voice and behaviors toward others, I admired him and grew to love him, really love him. I started calling him "Deej" and his subtle smile when I did so was his way of granting me permission to continue doing so.

Deej was getting older and taller. He still made capital Ds and resisted any opportunities to learn or practice cursive. He procrastinated on all writing assignments, because he preferred to stick to the facts, stating only the facts, in numerical order if possible.

DJ enjoyed a few explorations as a student, like learning science facts and mathematical operations. He liked piecing things together. I loved having him in my circle groups because he always had such interesting observations and unique perspectives about characters and story plots.

One day DJ's dad told me that Deej was going to ride his bike home (alone) for the first time. I could see he was a bit nervous about this milestone. He was as hesitant to allow it as DJ was excited to experience it.

Turns out, I had planned on an afternoon run, so I told his dad I'd run him home. His parents were always inviting me over, so I figured this way, we could get him home safely AND I could oblige their numerous invitations.

When we got to his house, DJ's dad was in the garage working on a car, which looked to be more of a hobby than a project. He was excited to see us and yelled for his wife as he wiped grease off his rugged hands. Becky came out with her strawberry blond hair glowing in the sun. I got the feeling she wished I could stay all evening. They were the kind of people that kept their hearts and their doors wide open. I was sweaty and ready to head back, but she insisted I come in and see DJ's room.

Deej had an uncharacteristically proud smile as he led me to each of his Lego creations, which were museum-worthy masterpieces. Once I went to pick one up and was startled by his snapping voice, *"Don't touch that."* It had been, like so many things in his room, placed "just so" and I was invited to look, but not to move or lift or touch. Fair enough.

I have this lovely memory of standing in the middle of DJ's creations, dripping sweat, with his priceless smile and calculated voice explaining intricate facts about each precisely constructed Lego formation while his mom smiled from the doorway.

As DJ was showing me the contents of a large, red plastic box filled with Legos, his sister, Sara came home from middle school and filled me in on her life since I'd last seen her. She was a bubbly and endearing middle-schooler, with a personality that was the polar opposite of her little brother. Her parents were quick to name the strengths of both their children and were the type to accept them as they were, effectively avoiding any temptation or urge to compare them to one another.

That year with DJ ended well, but it also ended with an unexpected twist. One of our 4th grade teachers was retiring and I was going to replace her. A request was made that I loop yet again with this class, meaning I would have nine students for a third year and DJ for a second.

By then, we had developed a closely-knit community. In a high mobility, high poverty school, you get used to students coming and going, so it was a gift to have a core of students to serve as a nucleus and as role models for the pillars of honor that we held sacred.

Even still, Deej had begun to withdraw from others, preferring solitude. He began to drift into his own zone. Many days he came to me excited to tell me about a family vacation or event, but more often than not, he came in somber, seeming lonely.

There had been tragedy in his family and they were all worried about the fate of his older brother. His parents kept me in the loop, they tried to stay positive, but I could see it taking an emotional toll on everyone.

I worried about DJ's grades and noted the quality of his work was not demonstrating growth at the same rate as his peers. In spite of extra efforts and interventions, Deej was falling behind and I thought about referring him for Special Educational services. The family did not wish to go that route at that time, and I understood their concerns, so we put things on hold.

I read a couple books about successful people with autism and whenever I'd share what I'd read with DJ, he would lean in and want to hear more. He told me he felt like he could relate. He had a special ability to zero in on certain things and was easily overwhelmed by others, particularly in social settings.

DJ started wearing a lot of camouflage that year and he often walked rigidly, as if he were a soldier. As I recall, he wanted to be in the armed forces when he got older.

Deej was a puzzle to me in many ways and at times, I felt like I pushed him too hard and in the wrong ways. He started becoming more agitated and sedate. I wished I could build a Lego bridge to connect him to his peers, to our community, but he drifted toward the perimeter.

As summer approached, I was worried about him. I hoped for the best, for peace as they weathered the storm that had ransacked their family's life.

The following year, I continued teaching 4th grade and heard from DJ's new teacher that he was struggling and that they were going to work on getting him special support. I had a new class with new kids to worry about, but it's always hard to let the old ones go.

Early one morning, DJ surprised me. He walked to the doorway of my classroom before any other kids had entered the building. I was sitting in my dimly lit solitude, hovering over my coffee cup and computer, checking email when I heard his soft, rigid voice:

"Hel-lo Ms. Wil-son." he said from the doorway. He was a soldier, waiting for permission from his commanding officer before entering.

"Hey Deej! How are you?" I replied as I stood to walk toward him.

"I am fine. I brought you this." His words came out in robotic fashion and seemed to slice themselves apart as they made their way through the space between us.

61

As he spoke, he held out a bright red plastic suitcase.

DJ stayed in the doorway. He was taller and thinner than I remembered him. His yellow T-shirt highlighted his pale face and his camouflaged pants were shorter—a recent growth spurt. His rigid arm was stretched forward, holding his plastic present.

"What is it DJ?" I asked as I attempted to close the wide space between us. He stood there staring. A young boy holding a red Lego box. I recognized it from the day I stood sweating in the middle of his room, the day he so proudly rode his bike home. He did not look proud any longer. He seemed dazed and lost.

"These are my old Legos. I thought that-- you could give them to your lit-tle girl so she can play with Legos." His words were crisp and his gaze averted. The box dangled awkwardly from his stiff arm.

I hesitated to take it because I worried that he would miss them and regret giving them away. I didn't want to take something so priceless from him when he had already lost so much in his short life.

"Deej, Are you sure? I mean, are you positive you want to give these away?"

DJ was a calculated person and clearly, he had already thought this through. He nodded in my general direction and made a valiant, though unsuccessful effort to look me in the eye.

"Yes. I am done with them. I don't play with them any-more."

I stepped toward him and took the box, which looked as worn out as the boy who held it. I was glad DJ wasn't looking at me because my eyes were misting. I quickly gathered my wits and cleared my throat.

"Wow. Deej. Thank you! This means a lot."

He nodded as I took the box from his outstretched hand. It rattled slightly as I lowered it and I watched as he left with an about face and marched down the long, empty hallway.

I let my tears fall softly, as I watched him walk away. He was almost my height, but in that vacant corridor, his silhouette still seemed small and fragile. He marched alone, always so alone, methodically, measuring each foot fall. A tiny soldier. A lost child.

As I type these words, my mind holds onto that picture, a young boy with a red Lego case, standing in my doorway. Tears pool and slide down the sides of my face. I let them fall and I do not wipe them. I know what has become of him, the little boy who liked to draw trucks and build Lego creations.

That was my last year as a classroom teacher. I'd been taking classes to become an administrator. I finished my practicum, passed my exams and I was off to be a leader in another setting.

The following year, I moved to the middle school, just up the street from DJ's house. I got to see my old students; the ones I'd spent three years with were now 7th graders. I'd regularly see DJ walk the hallways in full camo. He did not acknowledge his peers and rarely responded when I tried to connect with him.

He never smiled at school. Not once. I started to worry about him and made a point to check in on him during lunches. He did not eat in the cafeteria, as it was much too loud for his liking.

A loving teacher, who worked in our Behavioral Learning Center took him under her wing. He ate with a small group of misfits, who were in her class. He rarely seemèd at ease, but at least he wasn't alone.

When DJ had given me the Legos, my daughter was two and they were a choking hazard. That year, she turned five and she spent hours building tiny creations with the little treasures from the red box. Her vivacious and free personality stood in contrast with DJ's. I remember how precise and calculated he was and I smiled as I watched her imaginatively build something never intended. I wondered what DJ would have thought about it.

I had given up on my ability to connect with him. It is exhausting to be regularly ignored and grunted at by forlorn teenagers. But for some reason, toward the end of DJ's 8th grade year, I decided to brave another attempt to reach out. He was walking alone in the hallway, tall and rigid. I approached him and he halted before me. He looked straight ahead, stone-faced.

"Hey Deej. How's it going?"

He was reluctant to speak. He looked forward, transfixed. He paused to let in the silence, then politely replied, *"Fine."*

"Sorry to stop you in the hallway, but I just wanted you to know that your Legos live on."

One eye floated downward as if willing itself to gaze in my direction. I continued.

"Remember the red Lego box you gave me for my daughter? Well I just wanted you to know that she plays with them all the time! She's not as good as you at building things, but she really likes the Legos. Thank you!"

DJ's demeanor changed. As if he was emerging from a thick blanket of fog he wrapped around himself to make traveling through hallways bearable. He looked at me, as if he remembered for the first time who he was and who I was. I stood beside him patiently. He looked down at the tiles and then back up at me.

DJ was smiling. It was a small smile. A slight smile. For a soft second, he allowed the corners of his thin lips, (scarred from his cleft palate surgery and silent struggles), to curl upwards. It was the smile of a little boy who loved his teacher.

For a brief slice of time, he was once again a 3rd grade boy, the boy who was triumphant at riding his bike to his house with his teacher panting beside him, a hope-filled child who built Legos, before the weight of the world had settled upon him. He said he was glad that my daughter was playing with them and then he continued on his course.

That was the last time I saw DJ Adams smile. He graduated 8th grade and shortly after his 9th grade year began, he shot himself in the head and tumbled off of a bridge.

I wrote his mom a long letter and I attended his memorial service. I wished it could have been his high school graduation ceremony instead. I wish so many things. But wishes do not bring back a life.

In DJ's honor, I write these pages. He is but one unconventional student with a tremendous backstory.

Young lives like his enter our classrooms and it is overwhelming. They misbehave and we misunderstand. We do not know how best to reach out and our noble efforts are often rejected.

We surely cannot save them, so instead, we try to imagine the miracle they were when they were born and the person they would like to become. We do our best to make them smile.

"I cried over beautiful things knowing no beautiful thing lasts."

–Carl Sandburg

Chapter 5

José—*Hate, Hurt, and Hope*

"If you truly want to engage kids, you have to pull back on control and create the conditions in which they can tap into their own inner motivations."

-Daniel Pink

José Rios Lopez was like a vampire, only instead of sucking the blood of his victims, he sucked the energy and air out of the classroom.

I could feel him enter before I would see him. He came angry and jaded, hood up, slamming his books onto the table, always the farthest away. No eye contact. Beyond apathy, he brought in anger and hatred. One day, he dared to articulate this during a lesson. An enormous sigh was heaved and an audible whisper escaped.

"I hate white people."

This time, I chose to engage. I was sick of his mood, tired of the way he ignored me when I spoke to him, wounded by the way he shrugged me off when I sat next to him, attempting to help him put ideas down on paper.

"José, I'm white. Do you hate me?"

He looked at me for a fraction of a second, then stared back at whatever he always seemed to stare at. It was not quite his work, or the wall, or his desk, or anyone else in the room, but some combination of all of these things, which amounted to an averted gaze at nothing.

"Yeah," he said. *"why not?"*

"WHAT!" I exclaimed. I was weary of holding my tongue and biting back the urge to send him out of the classroom, away from the rest of us who had the decency to hide what we really felt, muting our most truthful thoughts. The last straw had floated onto the invisible camel's back and I snapped.

"You don't get to say that. You don't know me. You can hate me for as many reasons as you choose, but you do not get to hate me because I'm white."

He gave a slight nod. As if to say, *"Finally, a thought from you that isn't pre-planned."* This was an issue he and I would discuss later in our relationship. But for the moment, the nod was a recognition of my humanity. It was an invitation to continue. It was a sign that he might now, for once, be listening. Perhaps now, we could work together in the same room without one of us wanting to eliminate the other.

This book was inspired by José. The second half of my career was shaped by José. And ironically, when the first draft of what I thought was a presentable book was finished, I took a long break from writing. I felt done, perhaps even a little proud. Then came a dose of negative feedback, which I didn't know how to work around. I didn't quit the band, but I quit writing the songs.

When feedback on my first draft was originally offered, my trusted reader politely confided that my angle was overshadowed by my ego. She imagined the teacher behind the stories to be a seasoned trail guide, rather than a co-traveler. She said it seemed like the author knew what she was doing, had some sort of magic, or secret dose of gumption hidden up her sleeve, ready to brandish when difficult students brought their hardships with them to class.

José was living proof that I didn't know what to do. I could hardly breathe, or get through a class period without crying. I was used to being liked, not hated. I'd been an elementary school teacher who got hugs every morning. I had no idea what to do with an 8th grader's gang signs and middle finger. The only choice I had was to quit or be brave enough to try something else.

My friend was right. The teacher who wrote the first draft of this book did sound like she knew what to do. After all, the words, the pages, the stories, were written after the fact, once the successes had squeezed themselves through the darkness and the din.

But in the painful moments and months before seeds of knowledge and trust could take root, that teacher had no idea what to do for the students whose stories shaped her life. That teacher stewed as everyone's education was interrupted.

Some days, most days, she had a hunch she'd find her way, that everyone would survive it all and be better for it. She held out hope that all would reap the seeds sown, that love would find a way to present itself and that the same dogged determination that brought her soggy, sorry, soaked self to the finish line of a rainy marathon would take her to June--with lessons learned and student-teacher relationships in good standing. But, it was only a hunch. A hope. A courageous notion. Never was there a sense that she knew or had the answers. She only knew not to quit.

If you read this book and think I knew what to do or how to reach these students, then I have failed as an author. I never became the heroine the Hollywood stories portray, about disadvantaged kids with a shining star to light their way.

In lieu of a shining star, I am a troubled soul, who lays awake at night wondering what I will do tomorrow. I worry my lesson plans are old and tired and that my students will fail because I have not paved a path toward any other means. Worse. They fail because I let them fail--because they didn't try and I blamed their apathy on them instead of asking myself how the selected content and crafted plans might connect to their lives.

I struggle with the reality that my white world makes me look privileged and spoiled to students like José. The sorrows that shaped me are of no interest to those who fight to maintain their existence and their dignity. Stories of my past are fairy tales to them and when I bother to tell them to kids like José, I widen the crevice between us.

And so, the first draft of my book sat dormant, collecting dust. José's jaded black eyes faded from thought as I immersed myself in the lives and stories of other kids. I was too tired with the daily grind of education to push past my writer's block. I couldn't summon the energy to remove the elements of revisionist history imbedded in my first draft. I neglected to take the time to re-think and re-write the whole truth of my journey. The years escaped me.

In the midst of my slump, my path unexpectedly crossed José's. Once again, I was stirred from my arrogant slumber. And I sat down to write another proverbial song.

Enter José Rios Lopez. Take Two. I'd intended to stay in touch with him because he was a life-changer for me and I wanted to keep track of his life. I did for a while. Then I lost him. I moved to a site on the other side of town. He dropped out. And only 50% of the two of us cared enough to keep in touch. Our emails and texts were one-sided.

In the midst of my writing sabbatical, my old college roommate came to visit, presenting the perfect occasion for a trip to our downtown street fair. There we were, meandering through booths of freshly brewed tea, hand-made jewelry, and one of a kind bibs, pondering lunch. The inviting aromas wafted toward us from nearby food carts.

As I followed the scent, I found myself in the path of a street worker in a neon yellow safety vest, pushing a beat-up trash bin, brown arms stretched into black gloves, cupping themselves around grey handles of a mobile trash cart. He pushed the trash up the sidewalk like my neighbor pushes his lawn mower in rows along his pristine lawn. The street worker passed nonchalantly beside me and gave a nod.

I recognized the gait, his stride, the unmistakable familiarity of a beloved and long-lost student; I saw my José.

It took me a moment to inhale, to form a sentence. I gaped at the long eyelashes on eyes that looked like they had forgotten how to smile. I searched his face, trying to find words that could unite us. I was overcome by the unexpected moment and I stared quietly into the older, heavier, more sober version of my most memorable ex-student.

"José!" I yelled at last, more eagerly than I meant to. In return came a soft, subdued sound, muted by the heavy fog and the thick raindrops that landed on us as we stood side by side.

We had stood together many times, in many settings, with so little to say to one another. *"Just like always."* I thought. I wanted to give him a million messages, new and revised versions of the regurgitated pep-talks from the year we shared as teacher and student. I wanted to rekindle our dormant teacher-student relationship. But instead, I put my arm around him and introduced him to my old college roommate.

"This is José. He was my favorite student ever!"

Even as I spoke the words, I wondered if they were true. Or was I a fraud again, that José could see right through. What I meant to say is,

"This is José. He and I have known each other for most of his life. We have a very complex and complicated relationship that he is ready to be

done with and I will never be done with because he deserves to have at least one fan.

"He wants to let things go and I want to believe in certain dreams, even if and even when they are long gone. He was my hardest, meanest student ever and he sucked the air out of the room and the life out of me, but we found a path. We learned to see one another. We found mutual respect.

"I taught him how to say sorry and make things right. He taught me how to not be such a self-satisfied bitch. I taught him to see himself as a worthy learner and he taught me that I have no business teaching if I am unwilling to allow students to ask hard, thoughtful questions that make me feel stupid.

"He taught me that I am stupid sometimes, but that I am also a die-hard. He thinks it's okay to be stupid when it's honest and I realized that he is as die-hard as I am.

"We share a stubborn streak and we share a lot of water under the bridge. For some reason, I love him. I chose to do this strange thing even when he hated me. He is glad that I did. Sometimes I think, in his own conflicted way, he loved me back. Either way, this is my José."

I imagine my polite friend smiled and displayed all the niceties that she always does with everyone she meets, an endearing quality about her. She likes everyone! But in truth, I don't actually know what her face looked like when she met José. I have no memory of the words she spoke.

I was lost in past memories, searching for a path through them so I could figure out how to store this rainy street fair moment in my memory bank.

José looked at me through the corner of his eyes. His lips never parted and when he spoke, I imagined he had fewer teeth, for his words formed differently than they had when we last spoke.

'I'm not going to hug you like this. " He said and he shrugged, nodding down at the filthy gloves that collected our city's trash. It was respectful of him. I believed in his well-intentioned manners. But it also revealed the gap he felt between my world and his.

My heart broke a little as I absorbed the truth in our moment together. I wanted to re-enter my fairy tale, I wanted to be José's fairy godmother and turn José into the prince he was meant to be. I always saw him in that light, but perhaps that is what the problem always was. Me believing in magic, and José seeing reality.

I stood in the rain as I watched him push on, wondering what words I would later use to capture my current emotion. I couldn't decide if the words resembled hope or disappointment. He was sober. He was not in jail. He had a paying job. He was a brown man pushing trash through a sea of artsy white people. He was my student. My favorite student. Honest.

Honest was the word I would use to settle that moment in time.

Maybe that's one of the reasons the first draft of these stories failed to acquire their intended outcome. Perhaps I unknowingly wrote them to be more beautiful, cleaner versions of the truth. I wrote as a fairy godmother writing about her prince instead of a struggling teacher writing about a defiant trash collector.

Once again, José was my teacher. As he was so often in my classroom. Once again, he unknowingly called my bluff. There is little room for an optimistic, pie in the sky, suburban slant on a city kid. Shame on me for being arrogant enough to believe I'd be his hero. The only success I ever felt with him was when we were side by side. He didn't want a hero. He wanted truth.

It's as if José was shaking his head already at all of my feelings. He didn't hate me because I was white. He hated the fact that my white lens fogs my vision and clouds my ability to see a colored reality. I kept seeing what I wanted José to be, not who he was. Maybe that was a good thing, but in José's mind, it was a lie. He had no patience for falsities.

I could not change José's past or the defeated version of himself that walked through the threshold of our classroom, but I could change my mind about kids like him. I could change my strategies, my texts, my questions, my answers. I could change a lot. I could admit what I didn't know. I could tell the actual truth, which would open doors, bring regard, and make way for respect.

José was and is without a doubt, the student who had the greatest impact on my life. Originally, it was my intention to write a book about his life, but he would not have it. I was going to do it anyway because his story deserves to be documented, but I couldn't bring myself to produce something he specifically asked me not to. My dream was to have him co-author it…but some dreams take longer than we think to be realized.

My dreams for José required patience. More than most. More than I was able to summon most days when he was in my class. But I didn't meet José as a jaded teenager. I met him when he was five.

He was the firstborn son of a family from farmlands in Mexico, with street-gang influences in our city. His eyelashes were a mile long and his wide brown eyes would summon a stranger from across a room to come and take a closer look. He was an absolutely adorable, well-mannered and earnest kindergartener.

José wanted to be a good student and a good boy. He was both. Except that he couldn't read or write. His English was coming right along and he was on track for his profile level as he entered first grade…except in literacy.

I often walked by specialists working individually with José to help him learn to read. He did not. He could not. But he sat, patiently and good-naturedly beside each teacher, demonstrating eagerness and effort. He wanted it so badly. We had every specialist in the building working with him on these skill sets as 1st grade turned to 2nd grade and on into 3rd grade.

By 4th grade, José was reading…and writing, only he was several grade levels below his peers and he knew it. He resented it. Why did he have to work so hard when they could just learn! *What is wrong with me!?* He thought.

His parents had other interests and priorities and I would not meet them for years. José continued to labor in his work, but with a jaded and angry edge. He began resisting the urgings of his teachers, believing they simply did not and could not understand what it was like for him. And in many ways, he was correct.

José's 5th grade teacher was a friend of mine. As parent conferences rolled around, he pressed José to come and to bring his family. Alas, José's family did not come, but José came, with a notepad and pen.

As told to me by his teacher, he came in as a young professional would enter a room for an interview. He sat down and listened intently, nodding as if an equal, as if he was not the student being discussed. He left with his notes and his report card in hand.

José moved on to middle school and I moved on to other responsibilities at a different site across town. As fate would have it, I was later placed in José's middle school.

When I went in to meet with my new administrator and see my new classroom, I saw José standing outside of the assistant principal's office. He was older, taller, huskier, and he looked hardened by his past two years of life. Still, his giant brown eyes and forever long eyelashes glanced my way. No nod, no recognition. Only a chance gaze before they resumed to staring at the coffee-stained carpet beneath his shiny, white high tops.

"Hi José, I'm Ms. Wilson. I used to teach at your elementary school. I remember you. It's good to see you! Maybe I'll have you in one of my English classes!"

José lifted his head slightly, but did not respond. He no longer seemed like the kind of kid who would attend his own parent-teacher conference. As I would soon learn, he wasn't even the type of kid who would attend his classes.

José had been to juvenile hall, had been a ward of the state and was heavily involved in his gang. He had little patience or regard for white people. He felt a giant chasm between himself and the rest of our educational institution.

I recovered quickly from José's indifference because I remembered the wide-eyed, hard-working young boy he once was. He still resembled the eager kindergartener in the hallway beside his teachers. I must have been staring at him as I recollected past memories because soon I heard an agitated man's voice say, *"What?!"* in a tone that was less of a question and more of a threat.

"Oh, sorry. I just went back in time. It's my first day in this building, so I was glad to see a familiar face."

He stared me down. I waited for his response. I waited in awkward silence for a while before he slowly lifted his head to stare through me. Past me. Beyond me. His eyes looked angry and almost evil, as if warning me to stay away and to disregard our past affiliations. They meant nothing now.

Out of optimistic habit, I entertained a whim of hope for my part. I convinced myself that if he was in my class, I would win him over. I strolled down the long, linoleum hallway, lost in thought. The sound of my feet echoed in the vacant chamber that is a middle school hallway when no students are present. I wondered why I was here. I wondered what had happened to José.

Lost in circulating thoughts of disappointment, as the sound of silent personal dreams drifted farther away, I heard footsteps approaching. I summoned myself back to the present reality, which involved me standing in the middle of a dozen open boxes, trying to figure out where to put all of the items I'd hastily boxed up. How would they fit in with the old things left behind? How would I navigate this new professional endeavor? The pitter patter of dainty footsteps grew louder and an elderly woman appeared in my doorway.

"Hi Ms. Wilson. My name is Marilyn and I am José's guardian. I came to say thank you for what you said to José in the office. José came to us from a juvenile detention facility. He was to become a ward of the state after his parents were deemed unfit to raise him. My husband and I live next door and watched him grow up. We just couldn't bear to see him become a ward of the state, so we decided to take him in. We are working with the school to reinstate him. Today we discussed his behavior plan. Thank you for being welcoming. I think José is really nervous about coming back. He did not do well here before and we are hoping for a new start."

I smiled, trying to sound confident and reassuring. *"Thank you for coming down and introducing yourself. I knew José when he was a little boy too. I hope to help him find himself again."*

That sounded like the right thing to say. But I had no idea what that actually meant. Who was José before, besides a beautiful brown-eyed boy? I didn't really know him. And who was I to "help" him find himself when I couldn't even find myself?

I don't exactly remember when or why, but at some point, I went back down the hallway to the office and told the assistant principal about my past with José and about how he was a little boy who sat diligently beside teacher after teacher with mighty efforts, yet lagging skills in reading. I told him about how José attended his own parent conference and about what a caring big brother he was to his little siblings.

The AP gaped, his mouth dropped open and he slowly began to fill me in on what all had happened with José since elementary school. The AP and I had attended admin classes together and there was a sense of trust between us. We both wanted to do right by kids, but struggled with day to day challenges. Budget cuts were looming and I knew we didn't have extra staff members to support José the way we needed to, so I suggested that he put José into my classroom.

"But he isn't in any of the English levels you teach."

"I know. It's okay. I can adjust my instruction to meet his needs. C'mon. We both know what kind of teacher he is going to need if he is going to make it in this school. I don't want to see him get kicked out again and he really struggles in English. Please, just let me take him."

And so, the words of the eternal optimist had been spoken and the dutiful deed of the schedule-maker had been done. José was put into my

English class and I quickly learned this was not going to be the success story I had imagined.

José sucked the life from our classroom.

Without even looking up, I could feel him enter, with a dismal sense of doom. His anger was deep and dark, like a black stratus cloud covering the sun, causing you to forget that somewhere it might actually be shining.

José would enter without ever looking up. He would walk to the table farthest away and slam down his books. He would either put his face down on his desk, or cover it with his hoodie. His very presence put me on edge.

There was no reprieve for that 56-minute time block. He was there on time every day, thanks to his guardians, (who he referred to as his "white parents"). He was present, but he was not really there. Sometimes he'd have his earbuds in and when I'd ask for him to remove them, he'd say, *"Why?"*

When I would site the school rule regarding electronics, he'd shrug. I'd repeat my request patiently and he'd utter swear words under his breath and make a begrudged motion to pull them out.

Sometimes he didn't.

I didn't even touch the fact that hoods and hats were also not allowed. He could listen with a hood on, but he didn't seem to listen. He sat there sketching gang letters onto his notebook. (Also against school rules). It was pretty much one thing after another.

I'd say, *"José, what do you think about the character in our story?"*

"Huh."

"Well, what do you think motivates him? Do you think he will make changes?"

"I don't know."

And I kept asking. During work time, I'd sit next to him and all but write in his interactive journal for him. Then I'd write long responses back to him. I could only hope that he read them and that he found meaning in them.

One day, I worked up the courage to ask him to move into our discussion circle instead of sitting face down at the back table.

"Why?"

"Because I want to hear what you have to say about what we are reading and thinking about."

"I don't have anything to say."

"I think you do."

"I don't want to."

"I know, but I want you to."

"Fine." He sighed, picked up his books, moved forward and slammed them down, propping his crossed arms on top of them to form a nest for his forehead. He pulled his red hood over his head and ignored me the rest of class.

Dang it. This was hard.

I drove to work worried everyday about how to handle him. Every now and then he'd be gone, not because he was absent, but because he'd gotten suspended for one reason or another and he was in ISS (in-school suspension) for the day. I always visited him and took his work to him. He scowled at me. But usually attempted the work.

I hate to admit it, but on the days he was gone, I felt like I was an amazing teacher. We got so much done, the discussions were lively and authentic and the huge José-cloud was lifted. We all felt the difference.

One good thing that came out of my timid request for him to join our discussion circle was, in spite of his original begrudged response, he sat in his new seat every day after that, without being asked.

Every now and then, he'd blurt something out. Usually cruel, but truthful. I decided to celebrate the fact that he was paying attention and participating rather than address the fact that he made me want to cry almost every single day.

Then one day, I got down close to his desk while his head was down and the rest of the class was reading an article.

"José, let's read this together and talk about it."

"This is stupid."

"Why do you think everything we do is stupid?"

"Because I hate white people."

I stared at him, pondering my word choice and finally asked,

"José, I'm white. Do you hate me?"

He looked me in the eye for the first time that year, and without blinking nodded his head and said, *"Yeah, why not?"*

Why not??? Hadn't I demonstrated the patience of an elephant? After all, I'd asked for him to be in my class! And even though he sucked the life out of the classroom and broke every school rule, I didn't send him out or away. He sabotaged my lessons and minimized my discussion points and insulted my authority, yet I persevered through doubt and tears! And he could not think of a reason not to hate me???!!!

I said, *"José, it's almost time for fourth period, but I really want to talk with you about this. Can we meet at lunch?"*

To my extreme surprise, he asked for a lunch pass. I gave it to him as he walked out, a head taller and several pounds heavier than those he walked beside. His red sweatshirt faded into the crowd. I wondered if he'd come. I wondered what I'd say.

That day was the day life with José took the smallest of turns. When he stood silently in the doorway, I invited him to sit down. He remained standing. So, our first productive conversation happened as we stood eye to eye. I don't remember if our eyes ever met. I don't remember what I said. It was nerve racking to be in a room alone with José, even with both doors open.

I'm sure I must have asked him why he hated white people. I'm sure I must have explained that this is a form of racism, to hate someone before knowing them, based on their skin color. But I don't remember the beginning of our conversation.

However, I vividly remember the part where he told me he hated the books I chose to read with the class. We talked about all the books he'd been forced to read with white protagonists and how he resented it. I remember making a commitment to find more books with non-white heroes (a feat that turned out to be far more difficult in 2010 than I could have imagined).

Mostly, we talked about why I didn't hate him. I told him I'd asked for him to be in my class and I shared with him the memories I had of him as a young boy and I told him what his guardian had shared with me.

At this point, José sat down. I followed his lead and sat next to him. He teared up and after a long silence said,

"I feel like I'm swimming in an ocean and I just want to die."

I said, *"No, we just reached some land together. We are on an island and we are going to gather our strength and figure this out."*

He nodded.

I had my work cut out for me. I still didn't really know what I was doing or how to move forward, but I knew I had to hunt down, read and prepare different texts and I had to craft more mindful, deeper questions that penetrated norms and got to the heart of matters. In return, José took off his hood, sat up, and began taking notes.

As fate would have it, our 8th graders were studying the Holocaust. And José's guardian/"white dad" was a Jew, born to holocaust survivors. José found it fascinating that someone could rise from the ashes of life to make a new life. Through the course of that unit, José asked profound questions. He asked the kind of questions that I could not possibly have answers for.

José began coming in for extra help with his other classes and was demonstrably appreciative that I gave it to him. Once, he walked out of our class in anger. I stood there frustrated and offended, trying to find my wit and collect the desire to keep teaching. I was so mad at him for making me feel like I was a bad teacher. It never occurred to me that for him, to him, sometimes I *was*.

The phone rang and it was my friend, Julie, who was in charge of our In-School Suspension room. She had a soft spot for rough kids. She called to let me know that José had walked to ISS to cool down. I was angry at him for storming out, but relieved he'd stayed in the building.

That same day, José came by unexpectedly during his lunchtime to explain and apologize. It was the second apology I'd ever heard José give.

The first apology I heard José give was when I had to apologize to him for not being more culturally aware when selecting texts for our primarily Latino class. He knew he needed to apologize to me for saying I was a shitty teacher, but he didn't know how. I started in,

"José, I'm really sorry that I wasn't more considerate of the backgrounds and culture of my students when I was planning our lessons. I want you to know I'm working on it."

"Yeah. It's okay. I'm sorry too. Or whatever."

I laughed. *"That was a weak apology, José."*

He agreed, but explained that I should feel honored because he doesn't usually apologize.

"Obviously. But it's a start."

His smile faded and a serious expression took its place. *"You know I don't hate all white people. It's just white people have it so easy and they don't even know it."*

For a moment, I wanted to be defensive and retaliatory. I wanted to explain that it sucked to grow up poor in a sea of rich kids and to wear my brother's old hand-me-down "Tough Skin" jeans, while everyone else wore Jordache. I wanted to tell him I spent most days hating my father and was secretly glad when he died. I wanted to tell him how bad I felt when he died, how hard I had to work to make it through high school and college and what all I went through to get a job when I was homeless, to move, to make friends in a new state. I wanted to list all my woes and tell him that I did NOT have it easy!

But for some reason I didn't say anything. Maybe a small piece of me knew José was right. Because although I could write a riveting novel about my childhood and the many obstacles I fought to overcome in my youth, I knew that wasn't what he meant.

What José meant was that I'd never be stopped by a police officer while skateboarding home from school. I'd never be randomly asked if I had drugs when I walked the street with my backpack on. I'd also never be called a "lazy Mexican" or stared at suspiciously when entering a store with my little brother. I'd never have parents who didn't speak English, standing on the other side of a river, split between two worlds, the one they knew as children and the one their children would know. I stood there finally understanding why he hated white people who didn't appreciate the fact that everything was not a fight for them.

José stared at the dark grooves that swerved in an odd pattern on the faux wooden desk. From the intimidating frame of a man came a child's voice.

"I'm so tired of it."

My optimistic teacher response was straight out of the text book of "What to Say when a Kid Wants to Give Up". Except one thing. This time, my words were the truth. José knew it. And he believed me.

"I know José. But you're a fighter. And you are not alone in your fight."

He nodded his head and wiped at the tears that were starting to form in the corners of his eyes in spite of his best efforts to keep them at bay.

We continued studying the Holocaust in class and José remained an active and engaged participant. He asked questions about the content as well as about the grammar in his notes. He was learning both.

We were fortunate enough to have a survivor come to our school to speak about his life experiences as a young man, from whom the Nazis stole his entire family, along with all of his possessions and dignity. He talked about coming to the U.S. to start a new life, how he learned English and became a successful accountant in New York. He got married and had children and grandchildren.

José leaned in to hear the survivor's words through his thick accent.

At the end of the presentation, the 8th graders formed a line and each was allowed to shake the awe-inspiring survivor's hand. José waited till last and then he sat beside him and exchanged a few words. The teacher who had made all of the arrangements for this visitation and who knew I'd formed a tight relationship with José came over and said,

"I can't believe it. This is incredible! I remember the day he stood on a chair, yelling profanities, while he flashed gang signs. Now look. He is beginning to see himself in a different light, a survivor's light."

It was the end of the year, and I found myself making an announcement, a pitch of sorts, inviting our ESL (English as a Second Language) students to come to an evening event. None of them looked interested. I added, *"The Superintendent is going to be there."* None of them cared.

Then José asked, *"Do you think the Superintendent really cares about ESL students?"* And I knew he wanted the truth. I assumed so, but didn't know our new Superintendent very well, so I responded, *"He says he does."*

José gave a nod as if to say, *"They all say that. But I'm going to allow my doubts in successful white men caring about me to persist."* Before I had time to think through the ramifications of my words I said, *"Then why don't you come and meet him and see for yourself?"*

José was 15 and had no transportation to get across our massive town in the pouring rain. I knew he wouldn't be able to attend, but I said, *"How about I arrange for you to meet him?"* José nodded in agreement.

Our district is gigantic and while I was on a first name basis with our previous Superintendent, his replacement was new and we were in the throes of huge cutbacks and on the cusp of a budget crisis. It took me till summer break to simply get a response from his secretary. At long last, with the help and support of José's guardians, we set something up.

The morning of our appointment, I stood on José's front porch to pick him up. He smiled at me from behind his screen door. His hair was gelled and the smell of cologne floated through the summer air as his guardians came out to thank me for this experience. They made polite small talk while José backed toward the car and waited beside it.

As we drove to the district office, I could see José was both nervous and skeptical, while I was characteristically, yet cautiously, optimistic.

We sat across from one another in the lobby of our district office and I told José the story of my first visit here when I'd applied for my first job as an Oregonian. I told him about how I sat nervously awaiting my screening interview. I told him about the interview and about the types of questions they asked. José listened with interest, because he had a new lens through which he chose to view me. He nodded. He looked around and I wondered what he was thinking. He probably felt a lot like I did.

Our prestigious Superintendent had the outspoken goal of making our district nationally known, so I was impressed that he took time to meet one of his 4,000+ employees and a student in her care.

When the secretary came out to get us, José gave a dignified, "Ladies first" motion and nodded in my direction. I smiled. He made me proud. Every now and then I forgot he was just a teenager.

José walked into the grand office, large enough to hold a board meeting (even though the district office had other rooms for such an occasion). The Superintendent's desk was a swimming pool of cherry wood, as long as José's entire living room. The Superintendent was warm and welcoming and offered us both coffee.

José declined and I followed suit. This was José's meeting, not mine. I could read José's expression. He was not about to take a drink from a powerful white male. He sat down upon invitation to do so and he sat far enough away from the table so as not to touch it. I could sense his hesitation to trust the situation. I couldn't blame him.

To the credit of our Superintendent, he was gracious and welcoming and made a point to be fully present during the dialog. Still, it was abundantly clear he had not met many students like José. He asked the kind of questions that showed this to be true.

I felt sorry for him.

This was a man who could speak at the state's capital in a professionally fitted suit and dignified lapel. Still, he struggled to connect with a straight-shooting teenager. I sympathized with how he must have been feeling because I'd felt that pain for months. It's the pain that happens when you are trying to be polite, but someone can see through you and will not accept anything short of a cut to the chase.

The pity I felt for the Superintendent's awkward meander as he stumbled through the conversation led me to speak.

"Thanks so much for having us here. José and I have had to cut through many moments of thick tension. I knew him when he was a little boy, but now he is a young man and he is seeing for himself that our system was not designed for kids like him. He is not sure if he can hang in there."

The Superintendent smiled, clearly grateful for a break from the awkward questioning.

I continued, *"I am very glad you agreed to meet with us because when you sit in board meetings with stakeholders who make decisions about kids like José, you can have his face in the forefront of your mind."*

He looked the tiniest bit surprised at my candor and gall. But what else could I bring to the large cherry-wood table with José by my side?

I pressed on, *"A few weeks ago, José asked me if the Superintendent really cares about students like him and I figured he'd appreciate hearing your response."*

The Superintendent had nice things to say and talked about all the special programs and awards at José's high school. He was kind enough to promise to stay in touch with José via email, and said he'd let his secretary know to alert him when he made his annual visit to José's high school in the upcoming year, so he could check in on José to see how he was doing.

When I asked José about it all in the car on the ride home, he shrugged and said, *"Whatever."*

I was upset with his callous remark. I had worked for weeks to arrange this encounter and had driven across town to pick him up to make it all happen. It was a hassle and this experience had taken hours. I wanted to hear José say it was worth it. Still, I guarded my tone and replied gently, *"José, the Superintendent took an hour out of his day to talk with you and learn about you. What do you think now about your original question? Do you think he really cares about kids like you?"*

He replied indifferently and without emotion, *"Depends."*

"On what?" I asked, wanting to defend the busy, important man who took time to talk with a troubled teen.

"On whether or not he does what he said he is going to do."

Fair enough I thought privately, then asked, *"Do you think he will?"*

José shrugged, but the look on his face told me he had come to a negative conclusion. The silent optimist in me was frustrated with José for his pessimism. But I could not fault him for being honest. Plus, when I really thought about it, I agreed with José's realistic view about how prestigious people too often let commitments and promises slip.

I hate to admit to being wrong yet again, but our Superintendent never saw José after that and they never corresponded. José dropped out of high school. He was suspended and perhaps expelled. Though I never asked about the details, I saw him several times afterwards.

Once, I saw him when he was doing manual labor for my dear friends, who owned a farm. They knew how much I cared about José and they cared about him too. They knew I'd want to see him, so they invited me over to visit. José looked healthy and strong, but I got a sense he thought I was disappointed in him.

That same friend worked to help him get into the Job Corps and he made it in. But they do regular drug testing there and I'm not sure if it was that or the fact that José got homesick or that his family needed him back home, but the Job Corps did not pan out.

A year or so later, I got together with José and his friend, who had recently (and barely) graduated from the same high school that José had dropped out of. They were both tied tightly to their cell phones and I could only hope their dealings were legal, though not much they did or said convinced me of this.

I sat across the table staring at two young men who were products of the system I'd served in since the day they were born.

At that point in time, I had moved into the very office that José was standing outside of the day we had reencountered one another.

What was I doing or going to do that would reach young men like these in a meaningful way? How was I going to make a life-shaping impact? Was I going to be the kind of leader who kicked out kids like this?

You want to know what happened to José? Well…it is fitting that I do not have an ending to this story. José's story is still being written. And so is mine.

He is an adult and a father now. The type of patriarch he becomes depends largely upon people like us, his community members and his friends.

When I introduced José to my best friend that rainy Saturday at the street fair, I said he was my favorite student. That is true. What is also true is that he was one of the best teachers I ever had. I've been thinking about and reflecting on the lessons he taught me for many years now.

There are certain people who enter our lives unexpectedly and they critique what we say and challenge what we believe. Knowing them will give us pause and cause us to consider new paths. Loving them will change us forever.

Chapter 6

Diego—*Gangster Dreams*

Bring me all of your dreams,
You dreamers,
Bring me all of your
Heart melodies
That I may wrap them
In a blue, cloud-cloth
Away from the too-rough fingers
Of the world.

-Langston Hughes

I grew up in the 70s, in the LA area, so I heard a lot about gangsters. I imagined them to be a dangerous lot, who went around shooting each other. I imagined drive-by shootings, stabbings, drugs, graffiti and theft. And then I met Diego. After that, my view of gangsters changed.

Walking into our middle school office one day, I overheard talk of police activity, frequent absences, and all the other things that administrators have to deal with when they are not evaluating teachers, responding to parents, balancing a budget, and running a school.

I was checking my mailbox and kept hearing the name, Diego. Out of the corner of my eye, I saw the counselor pop her head out of her office to join the discussion. She was shaking her head in a concerned kind of way. The question was repeated, *"What are we going to do about it?"*

I know. I know. None of this was any of my business. But I had just come from a rough school and I had taken a liking to rough kids. *"Um, who are you guys talking about?"* I asked, trying to sound more curious than nosey. I think I even attempted to act like it might be one of my students, so I would seem less like an eavesdropper and more like a concerned teacher.

"Diego." They all said, almost at once. Like they had said the name and sighed over the name one too many times.

"Oh." I said. *"I don't know him."*

"Yeah," said the counselor, with a face that shone of a radiant kindness tangled with deep concern. *"You probably wouldn't know him. He rarely comes. In fact, we can't generally get him here."*

"Oh." I said again, with a dozen more questions on the tip of my tongue.

I don't know why I said this. Maybe it was because I had José and because I figured Diego might be a lot like José and I really liked José. Maybe it was stupidity, or wanting to rise to a challenge, or due to my pity for the administrative team, who was spread so entirely thin, I feared they would become shreds of rag right before my eyes.

And so, without really thinking about what it would mean and without really knowing where it would take me and without really having an end goal or first step in mind, I said, *"You can put him in my class."*

Same song, second verse. My favorite assistant principal looked at me as if to say, *"Are you sure?" "He's not in your English level."* and *"Good luck."* All at once.

"Wait!" I said, not out of wisdom or foresight, but out of respect for this kid I'd never met. *"Is he here today?"*

"Yes. He just showed up. Late. And there is some news of recent police activity."

"Okay," I said. *"Before we make any changes, can I first talk with him to see if he wants to switch classes?"* The office team looked at me, but no one said a word.

"What does he look like?" I asked. *"I'll go find him and talk with him at lunch time."* My favorite AP took me into his office and showed me a picture of Diego on his computer. Then he thanked me for caring about a kid I never met, wished me good luck, and told me to let him know after I met Diego if I still wanted him in my class.

"Okay," I said as I dashed off.

"Christy." He called after me.

"Yeah?"

"You are so weird."

"I know," I said as I left smiling. And I did know that. But I also knew that if you tell a kid you want him in your class and if you ask a kid his opinion and you really care to know it, it will mean something to him. And by now, I'd gotten to the point where it was a personal hobby of mine to offer a tough kid something meaningful. Besides, what other options did we have besides to haphazardly switch his classes around? We were fresh out of other ideas on how to get his ass to school or keep his ass in school.

When lunch came, I set out to find Diego. He was at a long table filled with tough and intimidating-looking Latino youth.

Just about anyone can seem tough and intimidating if you don't know them and if they don't look like you or the people you are used to hanging around. Past experiences have repeatedly revealed that all it takes to build a bond is to overcome that first instinct to fear that which is different.

My heart has been melted a thousand times by the beautiful, gentle spirit of someone who, two seconds earlier, had made me feel afraid. And so, I looked up and down the table at these brown young men for the face of the kid I had seen on the assistant principal's computer. Most of them looked well beyond their age. Even with them sitting down, I could tell they were all taller than me.

They looked up at the white lady who approached them. It was easy to find Diego; I simply asked one of my students and he nodded at a quiet young man, who looked to be peacefully enjoying his lunch, amidst the noise and chaos that is a middle school cafeteria.

"Um, Hi. Are you Diego?" I asked, trying to sound as natural and composed as possible, like I always walked up to gangsters who were in trouble with law enforcement during my lunch break.

He nodded and added a *"Yeah, why?"*

I motioned to the space beside him and asked if I could sit down. I said I had a strange question for him. He smiled. Not a sly smile or a sarcastic smile. It genuinely seemed to be a sincere, amused smile. His eyes took me in. And then he shook his head in disbelief.

"Oh. Sorry." I said, realizing why he was amused. There I stood, dressed as a witch, black lipstick, black cape, black wig, larger than necessary black hat, with Diego sitting there looking up at me, like I'd just flown in on a broom. *"Um. Happy Halloween!"* I added smiling.

He smiled back. It was an inviting smile.

I liked him already. And I was already hoping he would say yes about being in my class.

It was neither smooth nor effortless to adjust my cape and witch's gown to a point where I could swing my leg over the long cafeteria benches, which were attached to the table, but I managed. Diego appeared to admire my struggle. And the whole time, I was thinking about the irony that I had to muster up courage to meet someone, so different from myself, at a table of "someones" so different from myself, when it turns out, I was the different one. Not just a white woman, but a white witch.

"Hi again. I'm Ms. Wilson," I continued. *"I teach English here."*

He politely responded. *"I know. You have Salvador in your class."*

"Yeah. Salvador's great. You guys are friends?" I asked, feeling relieved because Salvador really was great. Salvador was one of the greatest kids I knew. When he moved into my class from another school in our district, his previous English teacher emailed me to tell me what an amazing person he was and that she was going to miss him tremendously.

The minute I met Salvador, I could see why as he quickly endeared himself to me as well. He defined the words "great kid" and "pure heart."

One day, Salvador freaked out and confessed to me that he had smoked pot the previous weekend and it scared him as it had unexpected side effects. He let me know he was intent on never doing it or any other drugs again. Both of Salvador's parents were gone and his grandmother was raising him. When we talked about why it all happened, he started to shudder. *"I don't know,"* he said. *"I guess I figured I should just try it since everyone accuses me of doing drugs anyway."*

"What do you mean everyone accuses you anyway?" I asked sincerely, not knowing what he meant.

"Not to be mean," he said, *"but of course you wouldn't know."* He truly was the sweetest, hardest-working, most helpful 8th grader I taught, so I tuned in, knowing this was not an insult, but the beginning of a lesson to be learned.

"Do you know that almost every brown-skinned boy in this town that carries a backpack gets stopped at some point by someone asking for drugs?"

"Um, every brown-skinned boy I know carries a backpack. They are my students."

"Exactly. That's what I'm saying. It happens to all of us. Everyone just assumes we have or do drugs." He turned his head sideways as his normally positioned smile gave way to approaching annoyance.

"Are you serious?" I asked as I looked at Salvador's perfectly sculpted hair, the healthy glow of his skin, his tidy clothes and red converse high tops. He looked stylish and clean cut. He did not look like someone who did drugs.

"Of course I'm serious. I can't believe you didn't know that," he said as his annoyance was giving way to encroaching anger.

"Well, now I do." I said softly, wanting to quiet the emotions of the moment. *"I'm sorry for my ignorance."* I added, seeing his gracious demeanor beginning to return. *"I'm glad to know now and I'm sorry that this is your reality."*

My memory of Salvador faded as I looked back at Diego, who nodded about knowing Salvador while he chewed his sandwich. I knew better than to lie about why I was there and I certainly knew better than to act like it was anything other than it was, a last resort because all the other schemes were ineffective.

"So, I was in the office earlier today and I heard you have had some attendance issues and some other issues."

Diego nodded again, with no reason or attempt to hide anything. He was not sure where I was going with this conversation, but was polite enough to hear me out.

"Anyway, the more I work with kids and the more I'm real with myself, I'm thinking we all have issues, so that kind of thing doesn't get to me. I'm sure you have your reasons."

He nodded again. He couldn't help but gaze up at my wig and witch hat. *Who had issues?*

"Anyhow, I teach English and I heard that is your hardest class."

Another nod. Then he added softly, *"All my classes are my hardest classes."*

I smiled. *"Unfortunately, I only have jurisdiction over English."*

He smiled back. Another nod.

"If you want, I told the office team that they could move you into my class. If that happens, we will have to change your whole schedule around to make it work."

Diego shrugged and calmly added, *"That would be fine."*

"Also, you should know, I will want you there. I mean REALLY want you there. I'm kind of strict about that. And I may hunt you down if you don't show up." To keep the moment from becoming too heavy, I smiled and added, *"You can run, but you can't hide."*

Diego smiled again, at the witch costume and at this whole entire out-of-the-blue episode. But, he might have been like a lot of kids who spent most their time feeling unwanted. So, a strange lady saying she wants to teach you is different. And maybe inside that difference is a potential for hope.

And so, I went back and told my favorite AP that it was a go. He messed around on his computer and a new schedule for Diego was printed.

The next day, Diego joined our 3rd period English class. I introduced him and we dove right into the business of reading and writing and journaling. Same drill. But not for Diego. He sat there, numb.

Fortunately, our opening routine was stress free. At the start of each class, the students would read from a list of affirmations and select one that was true for them that day. Then they'd write it next to the date in their journal. Sometimes we'd share out loud why it was true, sometimes we'd just silently honor that it was true. A genius idea I stole from a colleague.

It is a pretty powerful thing to have middle schoolers, beaten down by the woes of life and the daily grind of middle school, walk into a class and begin by selecting a positive phrase that is or will become true for them that day.

"I will not give up on myself."

"I will work hard for what I want."

"I believe in myself and my dreams."

"I can do hard things."

"I can overcome obstacles that come into my path."

"I will choose kindness today."

"I will respect myself and those around me."

"Hard work pays off."

After they'd all written their selected statements into their journals, we'd begin. Some days, for certain kids, this simple task seemed more important and urgent than the lesson I had planned.

I walked over to Diego as his pencil hand sat hovering over his blank notebook paper, shaking slightly. *"Let's get you started."* I said, as I grabbed the pencil from behind my ear and wrote the date for him. He watched in disbelief. *Had I really just come over and started writing on his paper for him?*

Yup.

Then I wrote what felt true for me that day. And I read the list out loud and asked him what was true for him.

"I will not give up on myself," he said.

"Of course you won't," I said. And I smiled.

He nodded.

"Now write it and make it yours." I said as I moved back to the front of the room to start the class on our lesson for the day.

Diego stared at his paper and sat still as a stone. I wondered what he was thinking. I didn't push it. I've learned that when you care, they know. They let you in when they are ready. And when sometimes they never seem ready, they still appreciate that you care and that you try and that you don't give up on them like everyone else in their life.

I don't recall Diego writing anything down that day. I wasn't going to push it. At least he came to school and came to my class and wasn't in trouble.

I don't remember when I first saw Diego write something down, but I do remember being surprised for two reasons. The first reason was because his hand shook, like he was afraid, like it'd been so long since he'd written anything, he'd forgotten how. He was hesitant and I had to encourage him to actually make the pencil touch the page and move itself in distinct motions to create a word.

Little by little, his confidence increased and so did the volume of his writing. But I remember how afraid he was to spell something wrong, to write something wrong, to be wrong.

I enjoyed freeing him of that. *"Stop worrying and write,"* I'd say. *"Words spelled wrong and written wrong are better than no words. Blank pages are for people who have nothing to say. You have things to say. Say them. You have information to write. Write it. You can do it. Stop being so afraid."* I said gently, yet urgingly.

Then I would say something to make him smile, *"Do you mean to tell me that you don't think I have what it takes to handle a few misspelled words? You think everyone who writes for me knows what they are saying and how to say it, much less, how to spell it?! If that were the case, they'd fire me because everyone would already know everything and what'd be the point of coming to school?"*

He'd smile. He was afraid and he knew I knew it. He appreciated that I put it on myself and that I released him from having to admit it.

The second reason Diego's writing surprised me was because it was beautiful. His letters were light and swift and beautifully formed. *Where did a gangster kid learn to write like that?* I wondered and I supposed he learned it in the same place almost every kid learns to write, in elementary school. His teachers had taught him well and he had learned well. *What changed in his life to make him the kind of kid that makes an entire office team worry about him?* I wondered. *Did his elementary school teachers worry about him?* I would soon learn answers to these questions and answers to a few others as well.

One day, a couple of weeks later, Diego stopped coming to school again. I tried calling, but I never got an answer. *Dang it.* We were moving forward and I didn't want to lose Diego. I went to my favorite AP and asked about going to Diego's apartment to see what was going on. The AP had gone a few times and warned me that he would not answer.

I had an idea. My good friend was our community liaison and she agreed to go with me. Before we went over there, I called and left him a message saying I had something for him and to please answer the door when I came. Then I wrote him a Thanksgiving card and brought it with me. I figured gangsters don't get many Thanksgiving cards and also it was something besides a truancy slip to have in my hand.

My liaison friend, Nora, and I had to navigate our way around many small lakes because it had been raining for days and the parking lot did not drain well. At the foot of the stairs, there was a rather large pooling of water and we stood there for at least 30 seconds, trying to figure out how we could get from where we were standing to the first stair without completely saturating our shoes. I thought sympathetically, *No wonder Diego doesn't want to leave his house, he practically has to swim out.*

When we finally reached his door, he answered politely. Diego was always so polite. Along with his gentle voice came soft features. The humble two-bedroom apartment looked like it had been straightened up nicely. It smelled of freshly cooked garlic and I could hear a sizzling sound coming from a pan on the stove. There was steam rising above it and in front of it was a very large woman, stirring the contents of the pan. I imagined that she must be Diego's mom. But I imagined wrong.

When I asked Diego, he shook his head and shivered. *"Hell no,"* he said. *"I don't even know her. My mom rented out my room to her."*

"Where do you sleep?" I asked as I looked around at the tiny arrangement of rooms and quickly added up the number of people who were living there.

"Right here," he said, patting the couch we were seated on.

"Where do you keep your stuff?" I pressed, realizing I was crossing into the realm of being nosey.

"Right there," he said, pointing to a very small space with a few folded clothes and some school books.

"I'm kind of out of clean school clothes and it's a hassle to get to the laundry room."

"Yeah," I said sympathetically. *"We had to navigate around the small lake at the foot of your stairs."*

"Seriously. I know." He shook his head as if in disbelief that we persevered through it to get to his front door. *"It's been flooding a lot and we complain to the manager, but he doesn't care. We are low-income renters, so he knows we can't do anything about it."*

"That sucks," I said. Because it did and also because everything else Diego had told me also sucked. Seriously, in my whole life I didn't know anyone whose mom rented out their room to a complete stranger and I didn't have any friends (besides in college when we were all crazy and poor enough to sleep anywhere) who slept on a couch every night.

I could see that Diego was pleased that we had come. He was the opposite of embarrassed. He showed me the room where his mom and sister slept. He wasn't sure where his mom was at the moment.

I couldn't help myself from asking about his dad.

"He and my uncle, his brother, are both in jail," he answered solemnly, reverently.

"Oh," I said, not knowing what else to say. *"I'm sorry."*

"It's okay. I'm used to it."

"Still," I said sincerely and I meant it, *"I'm sorry."* I added, *"And I'm also sorry your room got rented out."*

"Yeah. I'm still mad about that," he said, shaking his head while also shrugging, resigning himself to his reality.

"I would be too," I said, as I nodded in the direction of the little cubby where he kept his life's belongings.

I changed the subject, *"Are you always so tidy, or did you clean up cuz you knew we were coming?"*

"I don't say words like tidy, but I always keep my stuff organized. I hate messes."

I thought for a moment about him in class and how he always dressed neatly and kept his work neat and his writing was neat. He was neat. I realized we had this in common and mentioned it casually.

Then I added, *"Diego, I miss you in class. I wish you would come back."*

He nodded. He appreciated the Thanksgiving letter, but he knew the real reason I had come was because of all his missed days.

The whole time we'd been talking, my friend, Nora, had been in the kitchen speaking in Spanish with Diego's new housemate while she cooked. When I looked over, I saw she was beginning to move slowly toward the doorway, ready to leave.

"We have to go." I said. *"But I hope you come back. Please come back."*

"I will. And thanks for the card," he said and his voice grew softer. *"That was really nice of you. No one has ever given me a card before."* He smiled and held up the card.

As Nora and I drove back to work, she filled me in on her conversation with the woman and had information to share about Diego's mom. I told her about Diego not having a room, or clean clothes, and sleeping on the couch. We both talked about the hassle of the flooded parking lot and what a shame it was that some of our students have so much and others have so little.

Our school had millionaire students, whose parents owned wineries up the hill and we had kids like Diego, who didn't even have a bed. *What would it feel like to be Diego and sit in class and walk the halls seeing wealth while living in poverty?*

What would it be like to sleep on a couch because your mom rented out your room? Or to have the two most influential men in your life in jail? All the while, walking through puddles that remind you of your poverty. You were born into a life of less, while others were born into a life of more.

The next day, Diego was at school and he wrote in his journal that he believed in himself and in his dreams. Diego kept coming to school through the winter rains and well into the spring.

During lunch, Salvador and a couple 8th grade boys would eat in my classroom. They preferred it to the noise and florescent lights of the cafeteria. Plus, it was two halls closer to the soccer field and they could be the first out when it was time to play. Soon, Diego began to join them.

Every now and then it so happened that Diego was the only boy who came. Sometimes I'd help him with work for other classes. Sometimes we'd just chat. I always noticed how he'd wash his dish and clean up his tray and mess so responsibly. He ate with excellent manners. When I commented on this, he told me his grandmother had helped raise him. When he was young and did something inappropriate at the table, she'd slap him. He smiled remembering it. I told him his grandmother would feel proud of him as an 8th grader.

He smiled and nodded. I told him I was proud of him as an 8th grader.

Some people may not think gangsters have good manners, but they do. They can be soft spoken and have gentle voices. They may dress well and keep their things in neat piles. They may also say nice, truly appreciative things to their teachers and notice when you care.

Diego, who we couldn't even get to come to school or attend class in October agreed to come to an after-school event in April. Our Spring Festival was coming up. I'd been working with the hip hop dance club and we were going to perform. When Diego heard one of the girls was out and that I was going to fill in, he said he'd come. I think he had other reasons too, like maybe he actually felt that this was his school now too and that he also belonged here and that he deserved to come as much as anyone. Or, maybe he just wanted to laugh at his white teacher dancing with the brown and black girls. Maybe he appreciated that our hip-hop club was a mix of all shades, with various degrees of talent, working in sync to learn something fun and share it with friends, kind of like school was supposed to be.

Diego came. He was sober and he seemed so peaceful. I commented about how happy I was to see him and about how amazing it was that we couldn't even get him to come to school during school hours six months ago and now he was coming after school hours. He smiled his tranquil smile. But it didn't last long.

Within days, Diego was missing again. I began to worry. Finally, he showed up, but he was not the same. He had gotten in more trouble, police involvement trouble. He'd been arrested again for some type of involvement in something or other at a local bowling alley.

He came in at lunch time, not to eat but to ask for my help with an essay that he needed to write for the Police Department, who was coming later that day to interview him. He was mad.

"Okay, of course," I said without hesitation, but with great concern. *"Show me the paper. We'll work on your essay together."* He took out a folded white sheet of paper from his back pocket. It looked like any other piece of paper. But when he slid it in front of me with his head down, I knew why he was mad.

I read question after question:

"What can you do to get yourself out of gang life?"

"How can you steer clear of gang activities?"

"Who in your family can support you with your efforts to stay away from gang activities?"

And on I read, a series of about ten questions.

"Okay Diego, we can do this; let's get started," I said, knowing we had limited time and that this task would suck under present conditions no matter how much time we had.

Diego shook his bowed head. *"I can't write about that stuff. I don't have answers for them."*

"Of course you do!" I said, willing him to raise his head. I hated the shame and the helpless feeling he held. *"We can do this. All you have to do is tell the truth."*

"But the truth is that everyone in my whole family is in gang life. How are they supposed to help me get out of it and keep me away from it? If I really want to leave gang life, then I have to leave my whole family and change my name. This is not a choice for me. I have no choice." He wasn't crying and his voice was not raised. He was an angry calm.

If the sense of urgency had not been hovering in the classroom like a dark rain cloud, I would have wanted to talk more about it. This was something I wanted to process. His reality choked me. I had no idea what all he was dealing with. For the past six months, I was thinking things were improving and here he was standing before me, suffocating in his own reality.

Under normal circumstances, I'd tear up at the senselessness of his situation and I'd dissect it from all angles looking for a sliver of hope. But these were not normal circumstances. Diego was still a minor, but it was clear that his interview and accompanying essay could sway things either in his favor or against him.

I knew Diego was mad and that he did not like or trust or care to be polite to the officers that sat waiting on the other side of the wall. I tried to coach him on his demeanor and on his perceived attitude going in, but my words were not going to sway him. I did not see his interview going well. There was nothing I could do about how that would go down.

As for the essay, I reread the questions and studied the defeated expression on Diego's face. *"Diego, we have to tell them everything you just said. They need to know that you did not choose to be a gangster, that you were born into being a gangster. How will things change if the people who make the decisions aren't privy to the truth? You must tell your truth."*

He shook his head. *"They won't listen. And if they do, they won't care. They already see me like that. They won't see me any other way."*

I knew he was probably right, but who am I if not a die hard for hope? *"Diego, we will write down your truth in this essay. Someone will read it. Someone might care. And even if they don't, it's the one piece in this process that you get to dictate. Let's write."*

And so, Diego took a long breath and sat down. We sat side by side, writing out the truth of his past and the truth of his present. I wish there had been time to ponder the truth of his future. That part of Diego will remain a mystery for me.

Soon enough, a staff member came in to get Diego for his interview. I nodded to indicate he'd be right there. We reread his responses together and I printed out his essay.

I tried to give Diego last minute coaching tips, *"Don't let your anger overtake you. Tell your truth in a way that helps you be heard."* I encouraged him to remember his manners, to not let his anger show as that would make the problem bigger. I reminded him that police officers are people too, no better or worse than him. I told him to speak his whole truth, that maybe it would help inform them for future situations.

Diego spoke openly and curtly, a rare moment with me when he let his anger be known. *"They will not fucking care. I know it. They do not care what I say. This interview is not going to help."* That was the only time I ever saw Diego act anything other than gentle. He let his good nature and good manners slip and I willed him to pull it together, or stuff it down. One of the two.

I, too, had my doubts about how just and productive the situation would be. Two of my neighbors are police officers and they are reasonable, fair and caring people, but I've also had dealings with a few local officers that struck me as impatient and arrogant. I remembered one particular officer who was unbelievably rude, sexist and condescending toward me. I hoped he would not be present. I also remember another local officer, who helped me tremendously. He was gracious, understanding and patient. I hoped he would be there.

Diego arose with a nod. He was never one to move abruptly or loudly. His mannerisms were so subtle and understated. I'm not sure which officers were there or what transpired, but I do know that Diego returned angrier.

After that, I saw less and less of Diego. He started writing gang-related images and symbols on his notebooks. He was jaded and disconnected. He seemed to go back in time, re-living the days when he did not feel he was a part of things and that school was not for him.

He stopped writing. He stopped coming. By the end of the school year, I hardly saw him. He had no intention of going to high school.

Over the summer, I went to visit him. Once again, I appreciated his gentle manners and enjoyed listening to his soft voice, but I also felt conflicted. Although he greeted me warmly and spoke to me kindly, I could see what was happening to him.

Even as we enjoyed the summer sun coming through the open door, there were kids below. Young kids. They were waiting for something and I did not want to know what. I got a clear sense that Diego was involved in something illegal and although I wanted to encourage him, I could not be a part of illegal activities. And so, we parted ways amicably, knowing our worlds were not meant to merge any longer.

Did I change Diego? Did he become a better, more successful person because of me? When I think about my role in getting kids to be college and career ready, do I feel that I did that for Diego? I cannot answer all of my questions about Diego because he is not done living his life. But I can say two things:

1. My life is better because I was Diego's teacher. When people talk about gang violence, I think of Diego, a young boy with a soft smile, gentle ways and impeccable manners. I think of a boy who had never gotten a card before and who was appreciative of every word I wrote. When I went to visit him that summer, he made a point to show me that he still had the card I gave him and he still had his journal, the journal where he wrote, *"I believe in myself and my dreams."*

2. Diego, wherever he is, (and I heard he dropped out of high school, moved to another town nearby, lived with a girlfriend for a while, moved back and so on); Diego, whether in jail, in trouble, or clean as a whistle, is living his life with the knowledge that there was once a white woman who cared about him, who was crazy enough to approach him, witch costume notwithstanding, and invite him to be in her class.

That woman navigated large puddles to bring him back, watched him shake the first time he wrote in his journal, ate lunch with him regularly, appreciated his good manners, helped him write an essay for the police, visited his home and sat on his couch. Wherever Diego is, he knows he was believed in and loved for a small spell. I bet my bottom dollar that, after all these years, he still has that Thanksgiving card and his journal, reminding him to believe in himself and in his dreams. I hope he still believes and I hope he still dreams.

Chapter 7

Dear Christian...

"I freed a thousand slaves. I could have freed a thousand more if only they knew they were slaves."

—Harriet Tubman

Dear Christian,

I knew you didn't ask for the life you were given. No one would have chosen what you ended up with. That's why, when I saw our administrators throw their arms up, I asked them to put you in my class. You had no idea what was in store. You thought your tricks of avoidance and sulking would wear me out and I'd eventually give in the way you watched it happen to every hard-working teacher and dedicated soul since the 2nd grade. But you met your match in me. I was as dogged as you were depressed.

You hated me, and some days, I hated you too. I saw your perpetual scowl and heard the swear words you uttered under your breath, and I silently breathed them too.

You hoped I'd kick your apathetic ass out and you could be rid of me. It was tempting, but I was as determined to help you find success as you were to fail.

You wanted me to hate you the way you hated yourself, the way I knew you hated me. I could tell by the long silences that tested patience, filling airspace and stealing time. Awkward tension rolled in like a layer of fog over an ocean. Your adolescent grunts echoed off our newly stripped tile floor, yet your words were inaudible.

I'd endure endless minutes waiting for your responses to questions I knew you had answers for. I'd stare for the hundredth time at the bookcase across the room or at the irritated faces of your classmates, who wondered why I bothered to call on you, to include you in our discussion. Although they had their own reasons to be distracted and disinterested, they sat in awe at the astounding level of your apathy.

I could tell your voice had been stolen when I first heard the scratchy squawk that emerged when you, at long last, finally summoned the will to speak. I heard the sound of a rusty car trying to start its cold engine. The key turned, a shudder, a rumble, click. Try again.

I read your mind, *"Why try?"*

I could see you asking yourself, without a sufficient answer, struggling. Turn the key, a stutter, a rumble, at last, words would emerge, creaky from lack of vibration. Still, an attempt, a response, hardly more than a grunt, but something I could hang a fragile shard of hope upon.

I saw you try to disappear under your hoodie. Some days I wanted you to disappear. You often tried to skip school, thinking we'd be relieved by a day without you.

Your sulking presence was a thief, robbing the joy from an otherwise functional classroom. It was tempting to let it slide, to shrug it off and move on with my lessons and the business they call education. But I couldn't let myself give up on you. Our relationship was symbiotic. Your fail was also my fail to reach you.

I don't know what in me gave birth to this notion. Maybe it was the fact that I got into this crazy business because of Jaime Escalante's work with kids who were not so different from you. Maybe it was something your mom said when we met earlier in the year. Maybe it was because of the potential I saw in you when you actually permitted a borrowed pencil to make contact with your borrowed paper. (God forbid you bring your own supplies to class and show up prepared.) Still, in those rare moments, I had evidence that you hadn't always been a failure at school. I suppose I was curious enough to see if we could recapture that which had been lost.

So, I went for you. You hated me when you saw me standing on the other side of your broken screen door. You hesitantly cracked it open at the sound of my knock. I'm sure your first thought was to close it in my face and leave me standing alone on the rusty porch of your rented home. You stood silently with the door ajar. My eyes scanned the inside of your living room, at the many shades of brown, the video game hook ups, damaged shades, drawn to a close. Your home was a cave.

Predictably, you were in your red hoodie. My mind's eye will always put you in that red hoodie. You loved to draw the hood, but not that morning. I could see your angry, tired face without interference.

I spoke softly, *"C'mon Christian. We are going to school."*

You scowled at me and mumbled something inaudible.

In my own way, I found a way to get you to follow me to my car.

You were taller than me and physically able to resist coming. All you really needed to do was shut the door. On some level, that is what I'd expected. But you, with all your rage and depression and angst were still too polite or too stunned or too curious to resist.

You followed me quietly to the car, like a stray dog - cautious, untrusting, and ashamed of being stray. Maybe going somewhere was better than going nowhere. You traded your den of despair for a shiny red car.

I remember thinking how different our lives were. I wondered if you judged me as you took your place on the leather seats. Did you consider the difference between my house and yours, my car and the dysfunctional one parked at the side of your house, next to the pile of trash beneath that dirty blue tarp?

I searched for something to say. All my words felt clean and tidy and ill-fitting of the situation I was dragging you from. You scowled as I drove and you must have wondered why I bothered to hunt you down. Did I really care, or was I on some type of a mission?

It was a school of 900. Your plan, if you had the foresight and wherewithal to make one, was to disappear and then drop out. Many teachers would have welcomed that end.

And your mom? What could she do besides worry? She had to work to live. And when she wasn't working, she was busy fighting her own demons of depression. She did not possess the strength to fight against yours as well. The weight of your world had worn you both down.

The silence haunted us as we waited at the stoplight. At last you willed your underused voice to form a word, one word:

"Why?" You asked as you stared out the window, watching the cars move in their various directions, escorting their drivers to distant locations.

This was not your world. You were a hostage, unwillingly brought into it. You never felt welcomed. You must have wondered if you were simply living up to the narrative that had been pre-determined for kids like you.

I didn't answer your question because I wasn't entirely sure of the answer. Was I simply living up to my narrative? *"Another teacher on another rescue mission?"* Were you my atonement for my other failures, for all the kids I didn't reach and couldn't reach? For those I'd misjudged and misunderstood?

Maybe you were my experiment, a litmus test for how successful I could be on my next mission to elevate graduation rates. Maybe I was a glutton for punishment. Maybe I had a soft spot for you because I actually believed you deserved another chance to be believed in.

I wasn't sure of the truth and I was done speaking lies. So, I waited out the light and let the silence hover, heavy as the fog that engulfed us. The dreary dank earth was evaporating and would soon give way to the warmth of our elusive sun.

Even now, I am not sure why I went to fetch you randomly, after weeks of putting up with unreasonable amounts of disregard. The competitive forces of my truest nature hint that likely, I was unwilling to be beaten by a 14-year-old. Perhaps my altruistic act was simply pride. Maybe I simply didn't want to lose, to return to the administration and tell them my experiment with you had failed.

What I wish the truth could be, what I wish I would have told you is that *you, (with your dark, razor-sharp scowl, biting words and long-suffering soul) are worth it.*

Whatever the reason was for my action of going to fetch you and your re-action of coming along, it changed things for us. Not drastically, but slightly.

Remember the first time I came to the cafeteria to get you? You hoped I'd forget or overlook that you hadn't kept up your end of our bargain. You didn't expect me to come to your table, where you ate, surrounded by peers. You sat there ignoring me while your friends pointed and nodded in my direction.

You had been told, just hours earlier, to complete a task. When you sat there and refused, the choice was given to do it in class or do it at lunch. Either way, I promised to help you complete it. You ignored me in class, so the alternative was now.

I'm not sure exactly what I expected you'd do, as you sat there tuning me out. But I was committed. I hadn't entirely thought it through. *What if I asked you to come and you didn't?* Then I would take your tray and start walking. If I started walking, would you follow? Only one way to find out. And I did. And you did.

You followed yet again, the same stray puppy that followed me to my car. Our footprints echoed in the empty hallway, you loped behind me, bitter and jaded, swearing profusely. Still, the fact that you followed gave me hope. Somewhere inside of you was a sense of duty, a curiosity, a hunger. You may have hated me and I may have hated you, but once again, I was more dogged than you were depressed.

Through the course of the year, we ate a fair share of lunches together while we worked on projects. In time, you no longer rolled your eyes when I'd approach your crowded table, state-funded free lunch in hand.

You started discussing your ideas with me and the sulking and mumbling of obscenities dissipated. A couple of times we laughed together as a story or memory would flutter into our conversation.

I would tear up when you'd crack a window into one of the sealed rooms of your dungeon soul. I saw the 2nd grade boy you described, the boy with the eager grin and confident hand in the air, the boy who loved school and held hope like a tiny bird, in his small, chocolate hands.

Then the bird flew away or was stripped of its wings, left abandoned by a father for reasons never told. That was when you stopped raising your hand, and smiling, and knowing, and looking up.

You looked to your mom and all you saw was a face of grief. So, you stopped looking. To protect yourself, you told yourself a thousand times that you did not care.

You found that you still cared, so you beat to death all the parts of yourself capable of care and you began your death march through life, waiting for it to dismiss you, to let you free.

That, dear Christian is when we met. You wanted to die, but you could not summon the will to kill yourself, for that would take effort and a plan and follow through. All the things you had relentlessly squelched in yourself. So, your breath kept your corpse at bay. You were alive, but saw no purpose in life. You were a child in the dark.

There were days I saw light, a spark, a smile during the lunchtime chats that you were too hungry to refuse. But I never saw it in class and never with your mom, and I think I was the only one who hoped on your behalf.

Your teachers regularly connected with me. They asked how you were and gave me work to talk with you about. They tried to reach you. They could see you were intelligent and capable and worthy, but they could not penetrate the barrier you'd created. Your thick bunker wall kept everybody out.

Then you moved…again. Your mom couldn't make rent…again. So, you left the dangling drapes, shades of brown, and tarp-covered trash. Away you flew on broken wings.

Unexpectedly, months later, you returned, darker and fiercer. By then, I had a new role. I was a student manager, who worked with kids and staff on disciplinary concerns. You looked through me. You tested me as if you had never seen me on your front door step.

You looked at me as if you'd never talked with me over lunch, as if you had never told me your story, as if you had no story. You were cold and closed. Your icy stare chilled me.

I tried to find you, to summon you back. I searched inside you for the light. I never found it. I do not blame myself for what happened next, but I do regret it. I still cringe when I think about it, especially when I consider it from your perspective.

For our last encounter, I ask your forgiveness:

You wore me down. No, that is not exactly true. I was simply worn down, beat down by the injustices of my job, the impossible task of fair discipline in a land of budget cuts and systematic inequity.

We had rules Christian. Rules that you and I both knew were created in a time that was not ours, for a population that was not ours, for a system that had not welcomed you. Still, they were rules.

You knew I didn't care about the hat that you insisted on wearing, in spite of the countless reminders to remove it. But it was a rule. I had to teach you to respect your environment. One exception meant I'd have to make more exceptions.

Asking you to remove your hat was easier than questioning and changing school policy. I gave you so many chances. So many.

I spelled out the consequences and you knew I was more than generous about the statement you were making. But at last, the final warning, the final request was given. I took your hat and you deserved it. You'd practically asked for it.

Taking your hat was never my regret. Still, every day when you came to ask for it back, my response was consistent, *"I told you that if you wore it in the building one more time, I would take it and that if I took it, your mom would have to come and get it back for you."*

Every day you came. And I'd say the same thing: *"You can have it back as soon as I hear from your mom."* I knew your mom. She had spoken with me at length about her fears and concerns for you, her only son.

The problem was that in my haste to make the hat problem go away, I neglected to think it all through. I'm sorry Christian. It was such a common action for an administrator to take. This blanket response worked on cell phones and other confiscated items, but it was unfair of me to apply this blanket response to your situation.

Keep the item until the parent or guardian comes to get it: An administrator's code. That's how we roll. You'd been warned.

Except, this wasn't contraband, this was your hat, your status in your world of loss, abandonment, and rejection. You were left alone to piece together your dignity and all you had to show for it was an expensive hat. By the time I had taken it, word was you were moving again.

I thought I'd see your mom when she came to sign the transfer papers. But, she never came to sign the papers. *What kind of a mom doesn't go to the office to sign papers to transfer schools?*

A grieving mother. Your mother.

I know Christian. I see that now. I see it so clearly, as clearly as I saw the anger and disappointment in your face when you asked, for the last time for your hat.

Damn that gold and black hat! It meant more to you than all your years of school (since the 2nd grade) and it sat in my contraband cupboard after you moved away…again…without signed transfer paperwork, without your dad, without your friends.

For the rest of the year I kept your hat, believing you'd move back, or at least come back. But you vanished.

I stayed for each grueling day in a job that made discipline impossible for kids like you. I knew that role at that time was not my place. I did not want a Code of Conduct manuscript to guide my thinking in how to serve students. I had come to believe in Restorative Justice and in being a champion for equity.

Knowing I would move on to other things, I began packing up my office. I placed your hat on my desk. I think a part of me hoped you'd come back for it, and in case I was out of my office, you'd know it would be okay to simply take it back. You knew I'd understand.

But you didn't. Your crisp hat, with the tag still on, was stolen by the one adult you allowed yourself to like. Since the 2nd grade, you'd been building walls and I gave you a reason to lay more bricks.

I hate the way we parted. I hope you will afford me a small measure of grace and know that I am making important changes. I hope you are changing too.

I thought you'd like to know that we're currently having quite the hat problem at my new school, but I handle it so differently. Rules are rules and I have to take hats, but I always give them back.

Also, because of all the love you never had from adults in your life, I give our repeat offenders extra love. I always smile when they hand me their hat and I take a stab at humor, saying something like, *"I take it as a compliment that you kept it on because it means you want to end your day with me."*

Or I say, *"If you need some attention, just say so. I'll notice you with or without your hat."*

Sometimes I say, *"That hat reminds me of someone I cared a lot about. He loved his hat as much as you love yours. He was very persistent."*

In my private thoughts, I sometimes believe in magic. Perhaps your hat made its way back to you. Or perhaps you realized you were twice as beautiful without it.

My biggest hope for you, dear Christian, is that someday, you will welcome back your 2nd grade self. And trust me, I tell all our 2nd grade teachers to never underestimate the impact they have on a child's life.

I tell all 3rd and 4th and 5th and middle and high school teachers I know, *"Kids don't drop out of high school, they drop out of 3rd grade. Then they linger in our system till they just can't take it any longer."*

I'm sorry you got to that point Christian, but I will never be sorry that I was your teacher. I hope you remember our lunches more than your hat. And I hope you find reasons to love yourself. I hope you find a way to illuminate your personal darkness.

Dear Christian, I loved you the best I could.

Chapter 8

David—*Apathy and Angst*

We, unaccustomed to courage
exiles from delight
live coiled in shells of loneliness
until love leaves its high holy temple
and comes into our sight
to liberate us into life.
—Maya Angelou

David Jimenez first came into my office as a 7th grader, so handsome, he could stop traffic on a highway. He dressed impeccably and expensively, despite his mom's limited income and the fact that there was no father on the scene. His mother always had boyfriends. But there was no dad.

David's mom had a minimum wage job and other mouths to feed. I would get to know her fairly well by the time David would be expelled from the school. I fought for him and pleaded with him to try walking on the road we were chiseling together through our conversations. In the end, he didn't. He couldn't.

First, I must tell you about the day I met him: Our first Friday of the school year, David entered our cafeteria with a posse of loud and seemingly entitled football players in blue jerseys. He wanted them all to be able to sit together at a front window table. He came to me to plead this cause, *"Can my football team and I sit at this table?"*

"Of course. Why not?" I thought. It seemed like a reasonable request as the students were all allowed to sit wherever they wanted. I hadn't realized that he meant can *ONLY* football players on his team sit there? And so I stood across the room watching a handsome, blue-eyed athlete create an exclusive table for blue jerseys. He stood at the head of the table like a bouncer, permitting teammates to sit, rejecting all others. I quickly shut that down.

That is how I met David. He was gracious enough when I explained that we can't segregate the cafeteria into cliques. He disagreed and rolled his eyes as many middle-schoolers would, but he did not push this issue further.

That year, David worked hard to present himself as "the guy who had it all," but I would soon see how powerless he felt when it came to making change. Apathy was his kryptonite. His heart was a tent, where apathy could hole up and camp out during the day. Apathy would bring lawn chairs and roast marshmallows and sing campfire songs on the dusty ground of his interpersonal capacities.

People who work with adolescent youth understand that this is a time when students focus inward and are self-conscious. It is not typically a season of life where empathy flourishes. But I am telling you that David took apathy to a whole different level. His excess of apathy crowded out the spaces where empathy could dwell.

Every time I ever asked David to consider another person's point of view, he responded ever and always honestly, admitting freely that he truly did not care about anyone else's perspective. The longer I knew him, the more I started to believe that he didn't know how to care. He never developed the necessary components.

Picture a handsome kid standing indifferently on a football field while all his teammates and opponents have taken a knee out of respect for an injured player. Everyone knows: When a man is down, you take a knee until he is up or safely off the field. That's what athletes who share a field do for one another.

Who do you think you are David Jimenez, standing there like an indifferent tree while the others bow? Kneeling shows compassion and humility. It is a sign that you understand pain, that you respect another's effort to rise after a blow, that you hope for the best outcome on their behalf.

David stood stoic until the verbal stream of angry words from his coach meandered their way to his distracted ears. He reluctantly, nonchalantly made a half-assed attempt to drop one leg lower than the other and impatiently waited for the game to resume.

David made no apologies. He never did. He would enter my office indifferently and no amount of explanation would result in his willingness to examine the perspective of a classmate or teacher. It was beyond aggravating, and I would summon deep breaths to guard and choose my words carefully.

One particular day, Mr. Antipathy rested on my round table with his head down, in the crook of his elbow. I wondered if at long last, he was finally *sad*, if the weight of it all had finally hit him. Nope. Turns out he was just bored and tired. Nothing I was going to say could pull any heartstrings.

Out of what must have felt like left field, I asked, *"David, what are your strengths?"*

"What?"

I repeated, *"What are your strengths?"*

"What do you mean?" His head emerged from the crevice of his arm.

"What are you good at? What have you always been good at? What comes naturally to you? What makes you feel proud and capable?"

"Nothing."

"No David, everyone has something. Everyone has strengths, the same way we all have weaknesses. Often our strengths in excess become our weaknesses."

"I don't know what you are talking about."

"Oh my gosh, David, no wonder you are so unaffected and indifferent. You don't know who you are or what you need. You have no foundation to stand on."

"I don't have any strengths."

I shuffled around my office and ended up beside David at the table, with a pencil in my hand and a paper numbered one to five. The title at the top: *David's Strengths:*

"David, we are not even going to talk about what happened or why you were sent here (again). We are going to make a list of your strengths. You can't go through life believing you have nothing to offer."

Just then, a lovely notion from one of Parker Palmer's books floated through the universe and brought insight to the moment. He has written many beautiful books, but the first book of his that I read was *Let Your Life Speak*. In it, he shares about fighting depression and about how he is no longer afraid of hitting rock bottom because he discovered that finding the bottom means you've found the ground to stand on.

I had an overwhelming awareness that the first step for David was to find a ground to stand on. So, there I was with the paper and the pencil and five spots to fill. David stared at me with a mix of agitation and curiosity.

After three additional attempts at explaining what strengths are, David shook his head as if to say, *"Lady, no matter what you say, I don't have any."* I didn't interpret the shaking of his head as refusal to complete the task as much as inability to recognize strengths in himself.

"Seriously David, you can't think of one strength?"

This time, when he looked at me and shook his head, the agitation/curiosity blend had faded into despair.

"Ok. Then we will discover your strengths together. What are you good at?"

"Football."

And so that is where we started. I told him to write *"football"* down and continue thinking and writing all the things he was good at. I gave him some time while I took care of other things. When I returned, the only thing written was *"football."*

I pushed him further and he wrote *"sports."* Nothing else.

"David," I pleaded, *"seriously, we can think of five things. We MUST think of five things before you leave this office."*

He looked at me like a parking attendant who has to tell you the lot you need to park in is full. With a look of vacancy and disappointment, he shook his head. He could not. So, we sat there, side by side, talking about what strengths are, how they are born or formed in us and how they guide us and anchor us.

"Why football?" I asked, and I kept pushing. *"What characteristics make someone want to get hit, knocked down, bashed into, and what makes that person rise again with sweat pouring through his helmet? What makes someone endure double practices in the heat of summer? What makes a teammate? Can it be dedication? David, are you dedicated? Determined? Do these qualities live in you? I see them, can you?"*

"I'm beginning to."

"How can these qualities, so necessary for the sports you love, also serve you well in other components of life?"

"I'm not sure."

I told David that *"football"* wasn't a strength. He looked at me like a kid whose favorite toy had been taken away.

I continued, *"Football is a game; determination and dedication are strengths."*

He jotted, *"quick learner"* onto his paper beneath *"football"* and looked at me with eyes begging it could count.

"Tell me why you wrote that?"

"I never played lacrosse and my friend asked me to play. I did. Now I'm the best one on the team. My friend, he'd played for years and I've only played a few months. I think I learn things quickly."

"What else does this example tell you about yourself?"

"I don't know."

"You were willing to try something new because a friend invited you to. What could this say about you?"

"I don't know."

"We have three things and we need five. You are not off the hook on this, but if you feel ready, you can go back to class. Whatever it was that got you sent here, can thinking about the strengths you offer this world apply to that situation?"

"I suppose."

"Then off you go. Here's your pass."

From that moment forward, David would readily smile at me and offer recognition in the hallways. He felt he had an ally in me. Unfortunately, this did not keep him from aggravating his teachers and being sent out of class.

All the many, many times he was sent out of class, I never saw one clue that he cared. But at least now he would talk with me about what happened and why and what could change and what could make it right. He still struggled tremendously to see anyone else's point of view, but we were able to add a fourth strength to our list: *"honest."*

"I'm not going to say something I don't mean." David said with an edge in his voice. He had been sent out (yet again) for neglecting to oblige a substitute teacher's simple request that he apologize for being ridiculously and unnecessarily rude.

"Fair enough," I agreed, wishing I could do more to mend the substitute's wounded ego, wishing I could explain away David's inability to practice basic interpersonal decency. *"Honesty is a virtue and in a world of lies, it's important. Let's add it."*

David's Strengths:

1. *Determination*

2. *Dedication*

3. *Tries and learns new things quickly (sports)*

4. *Honest*

5.

We broke for summer and the list stayed with my files. As an 8th grader, David came back even more lost and less grounded. More of his mom's boyfriends had come and gone. A locker room incident with a friend caused his friend to move away. There was some shame involved and it affected David even though he never spoke of it to me.

Then one day, as David sat outside my office while I finished up an overdue newsletter, an important "what if" occurred to me.

What if David had a disability? Like a Special Education student with a reading disability struggles to read? Like a student with Oppositional Defiant Disorder struggles to comply? Like a student with Attention Deficit Hyperactive Disorder struggles to sit still? Like a student with Emotional Disturbance struggles to control his anger? Like a student with Autism struggles to understand emotion?

If David were struggling to learn math, would we kick him out of math class or would we find another approach, explain things differently, model more, slow down our process? What if he had an emotional disability that made it a thousand times harder to empathize and see another's perspective?

I ran my idea past David. He sat down and looked at me intently.

"I don't know. But your idea makes sense. I don't know how to show or feel things like people want me to and I don't know why it's so hard."

We had a few follow up conversations about this and I began to partner with his mom in conversations on his behalf. We were making headway against hurricane force winds. But not fast enough. His teachers and our other administrators were done. Enough was enough. He'd been warned. He'd had chances. He did not hold up his end of the bargain.

The staff agreed to a meeting with David. David's mom, his school counselor, and all five of his teachers attended, including his elective teachers. We called these meetings "Staffings" and they were serious, meaning they generally carried a "shape up or ship out" message. We only called a "Staffing" when a series of other attempts and strategies had been exhausted and desirable change had not yet been demonstrated.

Just before David's Staffing was to begin, our principal called to let us know she was going to be late because the district-level budget meeting was going long. I led the meeting.

David and I sat side by side. I asked if we could open the meeting by discussing David's strengths. And to the credit of the dedicated professionals in the room, genuine notions of his strengths poured forth.

His teachers had wonderful things to say about him. They liked and appreciated him. But they were stuck between a rock and a hard place by his refusal to do as asked. They felt like messages were being sent to other students that it's okay to defy the authority of those responsible. They had other worries as well. He was academically capable, but not doing his part. He was failing.

The teachers had all tried reaching out to him, offering to meet with him during his lunches to catch him up, yet he kept pulling away. His efforts were slipping along with his grades. I saw it. I believed them. But I was heartbroken for David. He and I were getting somewhere. Still, his growth in my office was not translating into growth elsewhere…not yet anyway.

At the conclusion of our meeting, the principal arrived, and a summation of our conversation was given. She gave him a lovely message about how we all care about him. I remember her speaking to him about the advantages he had as a smart, handsome, athletic kid over others who struggled with self-esteem, acne, and academic deficits.

If she only knew that he saw himself as the "others" she described. David did not look into a mirror and see a clear-skinned, blue-eyed, able-bodied jock staring back. He saw himself as an unworthy, incapable misfit.

The principal and the teachers agreed to give him a final chance and they wished him well. They hugged him and went off to prepare the lessons for the day. David followed me to my office. We talked about the meeting. We talked about his feelings. He was no longer apathetic, but he was doubtful. He didn't know how he was going to make the changes they were demanding of him. I told him what I was beginning to see and understand:

"I now see why you dress so impeccably, always matching, always handsome. You think that maybe, if you wear expensive clothes, you'll feel like you have value. You think that if your outfits are put together well, you will feel like you are put together well, like a whole person. You are wishing upon your last star that your outside beauty can make its way inside. At some point, you tire from it all and begin to wonder if anything will ever be better for you. You wonder if it would just be easier to stop caring and trying. You wonder if apathy will make your searing pain lessen to a manageable ache. You want to see the world through different eyes. But you don't know how and you are afraid. I see that now."

David nodded in agreement and we walked slowly out of the office and down the hallway together. He gave me a final nod before heading into class and I crossed my fingers for him.

A few days later, before our handsome heartthrob with a heartache had a chance to write his fifth strength, his mom found me in the hallway. *"They're kicking him out! He's done here! They expelled him!"* I was blindsided, though not entirely surprised. You can't give a guy with a lifetime of bad habits just one more chance to not screw up and expect he won't.

I do not blame the teachers or the principal for their decision and I know why they didn't want to run it by me before making the call. They knew where I would stand. They knew I'd ask difficult questions.

They were right. The paperwork was on our principal's desk when I went in to see her about it. *"When is the expulsion hearing?"* I asked.

"Tomorrow is his last day." She gave me her "I know the way you feel about this and I appreciate your efforts, but we had no choice" look. I'd seen it before. And truthfully, I appreciated her efforts as well. It's hard to make impossibly complex decisions on a regular basis at break-neck pace, while being short staffed due to budget cuts.

I have no apologies for David. I just wish we had more time. I hate the system that gives only one option for a guy like him. He'd soon arrive at the school where the "bad boys" go. The message had been delivered. If you go where the "bad boys" go, then how else can you become anything but a bad boy?

I understand our staff members' work with David was an exercise in patience and angle-searching. They did their best to understand him. Still, when a student is voted off the island, we've all failed somehow.

Thankfully, failure is not without silver lining. It's a great teacher if we choose to see the lesson. But it's failure nonetheless.

David did not leave empty-handed and he did not leave in despair. He left with a list of strengths, with space for one more addition. That was the best foundation the two of us could have come upon as we learned to work and move forward together.

n students like David walk into our classrooms, offices, and lives, we ᴄ ᴀot predict the impact they will have on us, the lessons we will teach them, nor the way our conversations and encounters will shape one another. We do not know if we will fail them or save them or know them or reach them. We cannot know. But we build a sturdy platform to stand on when we teach them to find and live out their strengths.

I remember the moment I saw David lift his head from the crook of his elbow, which rested on the round table in my office. He lifted his head to look me in the eye, not because I asked him to, or threatened him, or issued him consequences, but because the idea of having strengths was new to him.

It is a worthy, if not far-fetched thought: Suppose we ask our toughest students to tell us their strengths. Will they lift their head and look us in the eye? There's only one way to find out.

Chapter 9

Grant—*Seven Words*

"I have learned that mercy bears richer fruit than strict justice."

–Abraham Lincoln

One day, during a rough season of budget cuts, I was asked to go to the local high school to support their admin team. Their principal was out of town and they were a bit short staffed. I found myself helping to draft a final copy of an expulsion report. When the principal returned that afternoon, I sat in on the expulsion hearing.

I had typed the young man's name and grade: Grant Evans. He was a junior. I typed his father's occupation: Tree Trimmer, and the reason for expulsion: Illegal substance use. It appeared this was not his first disciplinary encounter.

As the deadline for the meeting approached and we hastily finalized the paperwork, I realized I was more concerned about the accuracy of the document I was typing than I was about the options for this student. The report was finished moments before Grant and his dad arrived.

I found myself sitting across the table from them. Grant was tall and healthy looking, with sandy blond hair and sky-blue eyes. His skin had absorbed what little sunshine the winter skies offered and he had a humble smile. I noted his teeth were a bit crooked and I thought about how the occupation of his father might not have afforded Grant the luxury of braces.

Grant was moving to our city from another district and the purpose of the meeting was to determine if his new high school was going to uphold the expulsion decision made by his previous high school. If so, Grant would begin his time in our prestigious district at "The School Where Bad Boys Go," which of course was not the official name, but might as well have been.

In the end, the decision was made to uphold the expulsion term. Neither Grant nor his father seemed particularly surprised or disappointed. They understood. Logistics were discussed and papers were signed. We all filed out of the room with the understanding that, when his expulsion time frame was up, Grant would transfer from "The School Where Bad Boys Go" and be welcomed into this, his new home high school, hopefully in time for prom.

Throughout my years in the district, I'd known several students who were sent to "The School Where Bad Boys Go" and none of them returned "reformed." None of them seemed better or wiser. They just disappeared from their home school to serve out their sentence and then returned, more lost and behind and distanced.

I wondered how it would be for Grant. The look on his face as we exited hinted that perhaps he was wondering the same thing. That is when it happened: the thing that lifted the chin on a face of shame, the thing that removed the power of negativity and handed it over to progress, the thing that has led me to say different things to students now that I've witnessed the positive effect certain words will hold.

One of the assistant principals met him in the hallway to go over a few final logistics. When all was said and done, she shook his hand and said, *"I look forward to your return. I've got a good feeling about you."*

The words hovered over us like a rainbow after a rainstorm. *I've got a good feeling about you.* They lingered, like the scent of baking cookies, leaving a waft of promise in their wake.

Clearly the words were not lost on Grant, as an endearing smile emerged. It appeared that this was the first time anyone had ever told him such a thing.

The words were a gift, some sort of balm, perhaps the kindest, most encouraging words he'd heard in years. Grant glided down the hall. Shame made room for hope.

I stood there long after he left, wondering why we don't say things like this to kids more often, especially during a disciplinary process. We focus on doom and gloom and dire warnings. We want our pound of flesh and we somehow believe if the punishment isn't shameful or hurtful enough, no lesson can be learned.

Perhaps our deep concerns concede to fear and we say things like, *"I'm worried about you and your future."* I'm not sure this phrase will inspire better behavior, but it will certainly invoke shame, anger, or resentment.

Teachers, administrators and parents seem to worry the most and so we are best known for our warnings of the woes in store if our kids don't shape up. What would happen if we looked them in the eye and told them, *"I know this is not where you want to be (or where I want you to be), but you're going to be okay"*? What profound seeds would we sow by closing more conversations with, *"I've got a good feeling about you"*?

These phrases imply the student himself IS okay and that he is worthy of good feelings to follow. Sure, he's still busted. He's still going to have to live out the just consequences of his decisions, but now he can live them out with a thread of potential to hold onto. Perhaps in that thread is also an opportunity for the birth of a more positive outcome.

I do not know what happened to Grant after his months of expulsion, but I have confidence that he was welcomed back warmly. I went back to my regular job and he went on with his junior year. But that experience left me with a new notion as I worked through my own complicated disciplinary scenarios.

I accept the fact that we don't get to control the decisions kids make and we often cannot control the consequences that transpire afterwards. Still, we hold tremendous power to influence restoration by the words we choose. Watching Grant's entire demeanor change at the sound of seven words make me want to use those words more regularly.

When we are at our worst, most humble, insecure place and someone tells us they've got a good feeling about us, it will lift us, like a gust of wind, that separates stratus clouds, making space for sunlight to illuminate our spirit. Inspiring words do not change the fact that there are still clouds and setbacks, but they give us a source of light, and in that new light, perhaps we can find a different, more positive, more productive path.

You have erred and there are these challenges that come with that, but you are not a lost cause. I've got a good feeling about you.

Chapter 10

Vanessa—*A Lesson in Equity*

"Look closely at the present you are constructing:
It should look like the future you are dreaming."

–Alice Walker

As was so often the case in my role as a disciplinarian at a middle school of 900, I was multitasking. Vanessa had been sent out of class and I was in the middle of writing an Equity Speech for the board meeting that evening.

Equity wants what is best for other people's children as well as our own. I wrote.

It does not reward poverty nor does it punish privilege. I continued, wondering what Vanessa would make of the words I was frantically typing.

Equity paves a path to showcase strengths. It grounds us to a foundation, a platform, upon which all can stand. Equity values differences.

As I wrote the words, I believed them, but Vanessa would be a tougher audience than our school board, which at the time was composed primarily of educated white people.

Equity leaves no room for shame or judgment. I typed, wondering if Vanessa felt shame at that precise moment. I wondered if she felt judged sitting there as a strong Latina, staring at yet another white face of authority.

I continued writing while she dutifully filled out her reflection sheet about what happened to cause her to be sent from class. Vanessa sat beside me quietly penciling her perspective while my fingers clicked rapidly on my keyboard.

Education is supposed to be equitable. It is a ticket to a future that is dictated by work ethic and commitment.

Education is supposed to provide an opportunity where all attenders gain and share skill sets. A learning community is not strong when only a portion of its members can thrive.

I was beginning to doubt my sincerity with each passing keystroke.

Equity ensures that everyone can participate in a just environment, with rules that strengthen, not merely a sampling of individuals, but entire communities.

I began to wonder, *were these the same rules that got Vanessa sent here? Were they equitable for her? Was it fair or just, the thing that had happened just moments ago, when she was sent out of class?* I stopped typing and looked up at Vanessa, who was no stranger to me or my office.

She was patiently gazing in my direction. Her face revealed a combination of openness and hesitation. I read through her thoughtful reflection of what had happened. I nodded and smiled as I pushed it aside.

"Vanessa, what do you think about equity?" I asked, truly interested in what she would say.

"I've never heard the word before," she said nonchalantly.

I liked Vanessa a lot because she was always honest with me. She had been around me enough to know I always asked a lot of questions and genuinely appreciated honest responses.

I read her a portion of the piece I was working on.

She looked at me blankly.

I said, *"Well, basically, it means things won't always be fair. People who need more may get more and people who need less may get less."*

I explained that some people don't like the concept of equity because it doesn't always work out to be fair or equal shares. For example, I continued, *"You get $10 and so does he, regardless if he is a millionaire and you can't make rent."*

Without further explanation, Vanessa responded with a declarative statement and a story of her own:

"I agree with equity because we have a house and we do okay with money, but we struggle at the end of the month to pay everything. At my church, we learned of a family that needed $30 to make rent. We didn't want them to be evicted so we gave them what they needed.

Sometimes people need a little more and those who have more must share. It would have been a loss to our community for them to be evicted. They may struggle in some ways but they contribute in others."

I wish Vanessa could have spoken at the board meeting. Her compassionate, insightful words carried wisdom. The same girl who was sent out of class for being apathetic toward the day's assignment turned out to be empathetic toward her church community member.

My job with Vanessa that day was easy. I simply let her know that her classmates and teachers are also members of her community, that she is a valuable component of her learning environment, just as they are. I told her she had a lot of wisdom and that her stories and ideas were worth sharing just as her assignments were worth doing.

I nudged her to replace the apathy she felt toward her work with effort, reminding her that her perspectives in the class should be shared by completing assignments, not silenced by blank paper. I thanked her for her equity example and let her know that I appreciated sharing a moment with someone who understood what others miss.

She nodded and left with her pass in hand. I continued typing:

"Equity understands the value of all individuals, knowing each individual will need certain things to be successful. It is true people may struggle more in some ways, but they contribute more in others."

This snapshot scenario makes me pause to look at myself from the perspective of a student. So often, I am frantically multi-tasking when a student enters the scene, like Vanessa entered mine. These moments are freezeframes in wildly complex videos. I am too busy to watch my movie, but I know it is playing itself out on a big screen inside my soul, one scene at a time.

Someone like Vanessa says something profound and I want to hold onto it. I want to push pause because I do not want the crazy pace of life to steal the lesson of the moment. I want to absorb it, listen more intently to the words spoken while the din is silenced. I want to pull the snapshot into the light to look at the picture closely, to zoom in, and see things I missed when the reel was running.

That evening, I pressed pause on my life movie so that I could write down what Vanessa said. I didn't want the wisdom to escape. I wanted it to linger.

As I wrote down the words of an empathetic 8th grader, ironically sent out of class for apathetic tendencies, I am reminded of the old adage: *Sometimes, you have to give more to get more.* Vanessa's family gave $30 they didn't have to help a family keep their home and stay in their community. $30 is a lot for a struggling family to give. But they got back far more. They received friends and community members who contributed positively to their lives. I started to wonder, *what are we willing to give to Vanessa and what might we get back in return?*

I wish I knew what became of Vanessa, but I don't. She is one of the many student ghosts of my past. Years and young lives drift toward and away from me, like the sea's tide. Sometimes, my memories leave me with regret. But when I recall my times with Vanessa, I am left with a and perspective on equity. Her analogy left me wondering if I could look past the needs that students present in order to see the assets they bring.

I am no longer thinking about all the things needy students take from our system. Instead, I'm wondering about all the ways they contribute to make our collective community a better, richer place.

Chapter 11

Ric (no K)—*Seeking Honor*

"We must risk delight. We must have the stubbornness to accept our gladness in the ruthless furnace of this world."

-Jack Gilbert

Today my daughter asked me how my book was coming along. I struggled to explain how it begrudgingly oozes from my heart to my fingertips like a storm drain clogged with sludge. *How can I do justice to the students' stories I dream of telling?*

Last week, I found myself typing a chapter in my head as I walked to my car. It was about a guy named Ric. No K. Ric Carter was missing more than a K. He was missing opportunities and lessons and nuances. Ric intrigued me and messed with me. And so I began to study him, his expression, his motive, his aim. He had the tendency to push us away from our objective, to distract, disrupt, and generally frustrate those around him.

Ric is the kind of person who will not go unnoticed. He is amusing and confusing on every level. He tilts and teeters in his chair struggling to keep balance. It is impossible to ignore his large sweeping arm movements and the banging, scraping sounds as his chair slides sideways and crashes forward. Again. Repeat. Teeter. Slip. Slide. Scrape. Crash.

Once More. And again. This was how I came to notice Ric weeks before I met him.

Ric, no K reminded me of the Sesame Street song, *"One of these is not like the other."* He stood out from his brown skinned peers for reasons beyond his teetering chair and strawberry hair. Ric was a human oxymoron--endearing and aggravating. I stared at him and wondered what it was he wanted, what it was he needed, what that lost thing was and if he would ever find it.

He nudged his peers and crinkled papers loudly. They took notes and he fiddled. They shared their thinking and he interrupted. It wasn't that he was intentionally rude or unkind, he simply didn't see the effect his behaviors had on the rest of us, especially on adults responsible for instruction.

A couple weeks later, Ric was unexpectedly placed in my group. Prior to his arrival, my group had been so smooth. We'd become a safe setting. We had worked through our timidness, doubts, and fears. As far as middle school study groups are concerned, we were somewhat of a success.

Then, Ric's group leader became ill, they split up his group and he was added to ours. The day I got Ric, nothing was smooth. He teetered and flopped and joked and generally threw us all off track.

This group was an AVID group: Advancement Via Individual Determination. These were students who had perhaps previously been "at risk," who were taking their education into their own hands and hearts. They were becoming note takers, question askers, and active participants in their coursework. They were being coached by AVID teachers and volunteers and they were learning to identify points of confusion, ask one another questions to help each other unlock their own answers, reach conclusions and identify the steps that got them there. These students were learning adult-like skills, presenting while their group members engaged in inquiry, note-taking, and discovery.

All the students that is, except Ric. Each group member was expected to present at least one point of confusion while the others ask questions and take notes. Except Ric. He was in a world of his own, disconnected and fragmented from the peers who shared his table.

I did what I often do with students like Ric. I use humor and kindness as a bridge between my intentions and his, the needs of the group and his.

"Um, I like your notes. They are so neat and thorough," I said as I nodded at his nearly blank paper, which stood out in contrast from the information-filled sheets in front of others in our group. Ric responded to the humor with a head tilt and a grin. I could see the amusement on his face as he puzzled to figure me out. Was I for him or against him?

A troubled teen can quickly detect insincere attempts of adults in their lives because they've been lied to more often than they deserve and because they've seen the dark side of mankind overshadow the light. They have a sadness so deep and so wide, it clouds their ability to believe in good intentions.

I decided to extend the benefit of the doubt…Perhaps Ric's aim was not to sabotage our AVID session. Perhaps he had unknown reasons and challenging issues. Ric could see I wasn't a fake, but what was I to him? And what could I become to him? We both let those questions linger as the AVID session faded to an end.

After the last of the 8th graders had shuffled out the door, the AVID teacher came over and thanked me for taking Ric into our group. She apologized on his behalf, explaining that he'd worn out his welcome with the other group leaders and she didn't know where else to place him.

Turns out, he wasn't one of the "official AVID students." Ric was a kind of charity case that they'd taken on as a last resort. He'd been repeatedly kicked out of his classes, sent out so regularly that the school administration had tossed in their proverbial towel. They crossed their proverbial fingers too, hoping for a miracle. Nothing else had worked. By law, Ric was theirs to educate, whether they wanted him or not. And he was a thorn in their flesh.

The teacher went on to explain that Ric lived with his older sister, who had been an unfortunate witness to a violent crime that had killed his parents when he was just a baby, rendering Ric an orphan. A red-headed, chair-tipping, life-questioning orphan.

Kids should learn about love when they are young. Ric had never been so lucky. And so, he sat around day after day in a systematic school setting, with all his creativity and wit, waiting to be noticed for all the right reasons in the midst of all his wrong doing. His random shout outs and off topic interruptions had become an identity of sorts.

One day, Ric blurted an undermining comment to an exceedingly patient classmate, insulting her, *"I know it! That's easy. I can't believe you don't know it."* He turned to me,

"Can I just give her the answer?"

"No Ric. That's not what we're here to do. We are here to help people find answers--not by telling them, but by asking them questions to help them make their own discoveries. If you just tell her the answers, that is patronizing, but if you ask her…"

Ric looked at me with a bursting grin and interrupted enthusiastically, *"Have you thought about the fact that X is a negative number?"* And then he gazed at the whiteboard triumphantly while the patient presenter realized her error and corrected the answer.

Ric bathed himself in the bliss of this moment. He had unlocked her learning with his own knowledge. He had knowledge to give!

This blurt out was Ric's moment of greatness. He went on to wreak havoc, but the lesson was not lost. Ric had offered up a nugget, a gift, an opening. Ric was smiling when the period ended. I have a special place in my heart for the smile of an angsty adolescent.

That was the day Ric, no K, decided to like me. The AVID teacher decided to re-do groupings and Ric was put in a group of one, with me. Every Thursday, I was Ric's 6th period teacher and we became quite endeared to one another. He'd talk to me freely about his struggles and we'd study poetry together, among other things.

Each week, I'd arrive with whatever food I had left over from that day's lunch. Ric would devour it on the spot. So, I started packing extra tangerines and pretzels. Ric was always at the table waiting for me, never late. He'd listen as he ate and his smile would melt the frost from my day. Ric would tell me about his life, his troubles, his points of confusion in classes and we'd work through it all one by one.

One day, he was not there. He had gotten in bigger trouble than usual. The assistant principal had tried to work with him, but Ric decided not to be a customer. He was too angry to speak and felt he'd been treated unjustly.

With exasperation and agitation, Ric eventually recounted the story for me in its entirety. He did not leave out the part where he yelled at his math teacher, nor the moment he broke a writing implement in her face, nor the moment he publicly ripped up his referral, nor the fact that he laughed in the assistant principal's face when he was asked to take responsibility for his actions. Ric made it very clear to me that no matter what I said, he was not going to apologize. His words tumbled out and gradually chased the redness from his face. His explosive mannerisms softened. He had been heard.

"Ric, you should not apologize," I said. *"Saying sorry when you are not sorry is dishonesty. But a wise person will consider the scenario from multiple perspectives. Can you be that person?"*

Ric gave a willing nod and quietly consulted his private thoughts regarding the teacher's point of view and the AP's point of view. He decided it was fair to acknowledge that it is inappropriate to take another person's things and break them. He also agreed that laughing in someone's face, especially one in authority, brings no honor to anyone and will generally create a separate problem.

Ric found courage to address what had transpired. He approached the AP and recounted the scene, explaining the motivation behind his actions. He'd felt taunted and set up, then later accused without being heard. That was his truth. He conceded that it was also true he had not handled himself with dignity.

The AP cut his consequences in half. But Ric didn't care about consequences. He cared about honor. He cared about who he was learning to be.

We educators become trapped in thinking that our lessons and conversations and consequences drive learning, but sometimes it is our mistakes and our willingness to learn from them that opens the heart and expands the mind.

And so, I wrote about Ric in my head on the way to my car because it was a long walk. And because as I walked, I passed hundreds of middle schoolers headed home for the day. How many Rics are out there? What if my own kid became a Ric? What would I want for her? What are the stories behind our students? If we as educators knew them, what would it change? How big exactly is this bridge we must build? Where will it begin and where will it lead?

And so, in honor of Ric, and in response to my daughter's question, *"How is your book coming?"* I opened up my laptop and I opened up my heart and I started to type, hoping my words might build a bridge that forms a path over our rough and murky waters in education--a path of learning, a path of understanding, a path that helps us hear our students' stories. Not to "save" them, but to reach them.

Chapter 12

Pablo—*Truancy and Truth*

*"The fundamental hypothesis is that human beings are happier, more cooperative and productive, and more likely to make positive changes in their behavior when those in positions of authority do things **with** them, rather than **to** or **for** them."*

-Laura Mirsky, Steve Korr, "Restoring Community and Trust," *Principal Leadership*

One morning, a teacher asked me what to do about a certain student. He listed the many things he'd tried and all his reasons for being concerned and annoyed. I responded sympathetically to all that he said, knowing this particular 8th grader had been a puzzle to his teachers since the day I met him as a 2nd grader. Still, I knew the young man responded well to both humor and to genuine regard, so I answered my colleague with a challenge, *"Put three of his strengths, three virtues, or three assets you know that he has in the front of your mind. When you see him, think about those."* My colleague nodded thoughtfully, and I added, *"If you can, find a way to tell him."*

Later that week, I saw that teacher walking down the hallway side by side with his student of concern. I got a sense that they were having a mutually productive conversation.

Interactions like these give me hope that we can find ways to support our students and teachers who are at risk of burn out. In our high-stakes, data-rich reality, we sometimes lose sight of the lives and the stories behind the data.

That same year, in my role as student manager, I had to unexpectedly cover for a teacher. Shortly after I arrived, a student named Pablo arrived late, with a pass showing 20 minutes unaccounted for. He was the kind of student that teachers have meetings about. His academic performance suffered along with his conduct. He had mostly Fs and he was sent regularly to my office. He and I understood one another, which is why he could not look me in the eye when he handed me the hall pass.

When the period ended, Pablo and I walked to my office to talk more about where he had been for those 20 minutes. We both knew a difficult conversation would transpire. When he sat down, I sat next to him, so we were side by side. I like the notion of facing forward together. With his head down, Pablo tried to explain himself. He stopped part way through, unwilling to lie to me. We sat quietly together.

For the sake of a productive outcome, I highlighted Pablo's strengths and talked about why I admired him. I explained to him that his grades do not define him, but his character and choices do. I told him there was nothing I could learn about him or from him that would alter my steadfast belief in him. I reminded him that his strengths would carry him through many obstacles. I reminded him that he could count on my support. There was an embedded reminder about integrity and punctuality and a brief dialog about the 20 minutes of class avoidance. In lieu of assigning a consequence, I offered empowerment.

As always, I gave Pablo the final word. We sat in silence for a few moments while he thought. Then, he said, *"Thank you. Your support means a lot."* When he stood up to leave, he had tears in his dark brown eyes. His parting nod indicated that the message received was not only, *"Stop being sneaky and get to class on time,"* but also *"Together we are a team and our successes are linked."*

Pablo did not know I would be covering his class that day. If he'd known someone he believed cared about him was waiting to greet him at the door, my guess is that he wouldn't have been 20 minutes late. Pablo is not disrespectful, dishonest, or defiant. He is a kid with a history of academic failure and personal rejection. He is sensitive, pensive, and courageous.

Pablo was later expelled for drug possession and I will remember that conversation as my last with him. I hope he remembers us sitting side by side. I hope he remembers feeling supported. We educators don't get to change students' choices, but we can influence their thinking. It is sad that so often judgment and punishment trump compassion and acceptance. We want our students to conform to systematic norms and rise to our lofty expectations without fully understanding them.

No way do I want a student bringing illegal substances into our schools and neighborhoods, but I'm not foolish enough to think a student like Pablo woke up one day and decided to smoke pot. Young people use drugs to escape from or numb their feelings. They are tired of fighting. *What if we worked as hard to address the feelings of frustration, anger, apathy, and alienation as we do to keep our schools "drug and bully free?"*

What if, in addition to searching lockers, we search their souls and help them find other feelings, stronger feelings to combat their pain? What if we painted a picture of future successes instead of continually stating our woes and concerns?

What if we told students, like Pablo, that we admire him and appreciate knowing him? Would he skip class and do drugs still? Possibly. But maybe not. And if you loved Pablo, if Pablo was your child, you'd do anything you could to usher in the best possible outcome.

Students like Pablo grow weary of failure and drop out of our system. It could be argued that they are pushed out because we are quick to slap on judgmental labels (like defiant, disruptive and disrespectful), and slow to see and encourage potential. We are sometimes hasty and irritable with students like Pablo because we are consumed with planning, teaching, assessing, and posting grades in a timely and professional manner, with documentation to back every mark. Their behavior and academic scores are recorded onto large data bases, posted onto spreadsheets, and become a standard by which our teachers, schools and districts are judged.

Meanwhile, the individual's innate strengths are lost in our systematic shuffle. Statistics trump stories because stories take time. They present a complex picture, which can't be categorized onto spreadsheets and data bases. Sometimes students like Pablo, and the assets they bring, are lost to us. And if our successes truly are linked, then his failure is ours as well. I do not pretend to have a systematic solution, but I believe that an intentional focus on relationships, strengths, and student empowerment is a solid start.

Chapter 13

Sharing Steve

"We look at the picture without talking
Sometimes, I don't know the words for things,
how to write down the feeling of knowing
that every dying person leaves something behind."
—Jacqueline Woodson

One after another the students and teachers approached the microphone, voices cracking, eyes watering. Stories were told; pictures displayed, songs sung, tissues passed. The desire to share Steve stories overwhelmed typical concerns of middle and high schoolers under normal circumstances.

Life celebration services are only a small step up from funerals on the somber scale. No matter how upbeat the slide show is or how funny the stories are, the same underlying sadness hovers over all that happens. It weaves its way through the aisles whispering a soft reminder that someone we loved has been lost to us.

In this case, it was Steve, a favorite colleague, a man whose smile lingers in my mind like the scent of salt over ocean sand. He was a man of integrity, with high regard for others. He was lost to us too soon. Damn cancer.

None of us saw this coming. He was a runner and a hiker, a husband and a father, a beloved teacher. But asbestos doesn't care about any of those things and Steve's lungs could no longer fend off the repercussions of past exposure.

Steve's lungs were singing lungs that gave him air to teach and tease lovingly. His lungs expanded the day he spent his plan time in the parking lot jacking up his colleague's car to fix her flat tire. His lungs calmly inhaled and exhaled in the middle of the night while driving another colleague to the hospital to save her life. His lungs gasped in joy at the birth of all three of his sons and powered the song of his 35-year marriage to the woman who made his eyes twinkle. His lungs were as amazing as his heart. Damn asbestos.

Steve didn't want to quit. He still had treasures to offer his students. And so, he taught as the treatment began…and continued, until he had to quit.

His lungs were kind enough to let him return on the last day of the school year to surprise his students. One final smile, a last twinkle, a gentle teasing farewell nudge.

Finding and sharing joy was one of Steve's super powers, right next to dropping what he was doing to assist someone who asked. I was lucky enough to be his colleague.

When I met Steve, I was a Second Language Specialist and he was a Science teacher. We shared some of the same students; one was a newcomer from Mexico. Steve, in his khaki pants and running shoes, would often stop by my room to ask what he could do to make his 6th grade science content comprehensible for this student.

Steve formulated projects and got information translated so that our new student could find success. Every now and then, Steve would come by, eyes twinkling, and ask for the smallest of favors:

"Hey, would you mind checking in with Marco, just to see how he is FEELING in science? His work is good, but I can't tell how he is REALLY doing. I mean, he probably spends most of class wondering what this old, bald guy is saying and I just want to make sure he knows that I care about him and I'm proud of how hard he is working."

The only favors Steve ever asked of me were on behalf of students. After one year of being his colleague, I became a student manager, replacing my favorite assistant principal in the throes of budget cuts.

In those years as a school leader, many teachers stopped by seeking advice and support. Their classrooms were overcrowded and the cuts to services and support ran deep. They had a lot to complain about, but Steve was never one to spend time discussing deficits.

During those stressful years, staff meetings and committee meetings could often turn to a negative place. People were overworked and overwhelmed. But when Steve spoke, however honestly, tension lifted. It was as if someone lit a candle or passed around chocolate.

I recall one particular meeting, when the climate issue that arose was our tardy problem. Students weren't making it to class on time and there didn't seem to be consequences that motivated them to make suitable changes. What was our admin team going to do to address this mounting problem?

I was at a loss, hurt and affronted because, although I recognized their issue and agreed that support was needed, I couldn't find a possible way to give or do more. My head spun as I tried to come up with a kind and genuine response. Thankfully, Steve spoke first:

"You know what I'm going to do to solve the tardy problem? I'm going to stand by the door of my classroom and welcome every student. If people are late, I'm going to look them in the eye and ask 'why?' We'll figure it out together. I don't want the office to handle it because I don't want my kids to forget that they are accountable to me first."

Steve had the same policy for kids who neglected to do or finish work, or for kids who misbehaved. He wanted to understand and he wanted them to feel comfortable enough to look him in the eye.

Steve helped us understand the jump between elementary school and middle school because he had taught both. He understood kids well and knew how to win them over. For one it was a song, for another, a joke, a nickname, a play on words, a timely smile, a check in.

One particular student used to roam around the room a lot. He found it hard to stay put. Instead of getting exasperated, Steve solved the problem with humor. It turns out, the boy's name was Roman.

*"Hey Romi (*his nickname*), I see you're roamin' again."*

The play on words felt friendlier to Roman than being corrected or chastised. I choked down a few extra tears when Romi spoke at Steve's memorial service, telling that story and thanking him for his endearing sense of humor.

Ellie was another who spoke. She was an extraordinarily responsible student, who shared a memory of Steve's disarming charm. She recalled the day she forgot her homework, a stressful event for an overachiever like herself. Mr. Lewis handled the situation by instantaneously bursting into song, impromptu and created just for this moment. His song was about a lovely, nearly perfect student, who was human after all.

Steve merged his sense of humor, musician's background, and teacher's heart in a way that made Ellie smile instead of feel disappointed in herself. He reminded her that the idea is consistency and effort, not perfection.

Ellie stood as a poised high schooler, thanking her 6th grade teacher for that moment in time and lesson for life. As I listened, I tasted the salt of my tears. I thought of Lincoln's words, *"I have always found that mercy bears richer fruits than strict justice."*

One by one, the voices of colleagues, family members, and students told their "Steve stories," and I wondered what mercies and rich fruits would bear themselves at my own life celebration ceremony. *How have I taught lessons that lifted spirits and made life better or different?*

I was struck with the sense that life is connected. My life connected to Steve's. Steve's life to the students' lives and now to yours, my reader friends, who rise in the face of challenges, driven by a desire to reach others, with the innate strengths you possess.

We wonder about our stories and how they will play out. Day by day, we are writing our own story, the one about how we didn't give up, even when we were furious, humiliated, frustrated, and insecure in our abilities to move things forward.

We engage in the stories of others as we listen to their words. We hear them speak their truth to the tune of their heart's song. We know that they had a past and that they will have a future.

We replace strict justice with mercy in the face of infuriating encounters because we remember that they are young and we are brave. Somehow, we know this awkward, frustrating moment will pass and that the relationship we form will last. We remember that soul-shaping work is not without hardship.

We find ourselves contemplating someone who perplexed or aggravated us; the student who humiliated, even bullied us, cowered from or avoided us; a colleague with whom we cannot see eye to eye. And we feel justice in our rage and anger for our cause.

Mercy sits beside us and whispers in our ear. It reminds us that life is short. Asbestos and cancer and life celebration services remind us too. Beyond our ego and our anger and our concerns, there is another life, also with an ego and anger and concerns. We are more alike than we are different.

Like Steve, we work and struggle and talk ourselves to a place where we can give the benefit of the doubt, just as we want others to do for us. We do the thing we wish others would do for our own children. We open the eye of our heart to see what is priceless and precious about them. Our ego breaks into song. Humor replaces hate. Our eyes twinkle.

Whenever Steve had the chance, he would pull the student aside and tell him about the strengths he'd noticed. He would ask students about their motivations and about their hopes. When they were jaded and angry with him over something he'd said, done, not said or done, he remembered that it is not too late to mend a damaged relationship.

We can do this hard thing, this best thing. We can apologize because we are strong and brave enough. We can explain why we did what we did and reveal what we wished we could have done instead. It's okay. We weren't our best selves at that moment in time and it wasn't our finest hour. But life is short, so it should be lived well.

DJ is gone because despair pulled a trigger and Steve is gone because lungs lost air.

But we are here.

Our life is long enough for us to love the people in our path.

Chapter 14

Sabine—*Unexpected Encounter*

"I've failed over and over and over again in my life.
And that is why I succeed."

-Michael Jordan

After all the drafts of all the chapters had been pecked at and fiddled with, read, and reread, I sent it all off to my kind-hearted editor. With a sense of accomplishment and satisfaction, I clicked send and set off about my business, waiting for a feeling of relief to follow. Instead, I was enveloped in fear and riddled with doubt. I began to question everything:

Am I a fraud? A hypocrite? Was I true to the students? Was I too arrogant in my assumptions? Maybe I failed them all and they are roaming the earth as I type, cursing the ground I walk on. Maybe, the second my book is published, my phone will ring and I'll hear a disgruntled voice on the other end, "Oh no, you did NOT do that." "You wish!" "Nuh-uh!" or perhaps something far worse.

Regardless of the result, I decided to celebrate the grand accomplishment of submitting five years of thoughtful work with a trip to my old stomping grounds in Southern California. As I was awaiting my flight's departure, I decided to treat myself at my favorite restaurant in

PDX. It was not a normal person's meal time and the typical line for ordering at the counter was non-existent. I peered at all the salads and soups and a smiling worker behind the counter offered her assistance.

She appeared amused by my ridiculous dilemmas: *"Should I get this soup? No. It has bacon. I really hate when they put bacon in soup...Is your clam chowder good? ...Yes. I can have clams, just not bacon. ...Do these croissants have filling? It's ok. I like them plain..."* On and on.

She continued smiling and I had to laugh at myself. I remained thankful there was no line and I appreciated her genuinely pleasant and patient responses to my plethora of inquiries.

I realized she was one of the special servers of life, the kind we need when we've had a bad day, or need to laugh a little at ourselves, without feeling badly about ourselves. She was one of the people who gets it, doesn't rush you or patronize you, but steps in to be helpful when you feel indecisive. I love those servers!

As I finally settled upon my order, she nodded at me as if to congratulate me on persevering through a tremendous struggle. Then she smiled even bigger and said, *"This is going to sound funny, but you look really familiar."*

I hadn't wanted to say so, because I was already taking WAY too much time to order, but she was familiar to me as well.

"What's your name?" I asked, returning her enormous smile.

"Sabine." She waited.

I responded as if I'd been prompted, with a name I had not spoken or written in over half a decade: *"Sabine Scolinos."* It was not a question. It was a statement. I knew who she was and the memories came soaring back to me like an eagle returning to her perch.

"How do I know you?" she asked, still smiling, but now, more timidly.

"You were in my office a lot." I said. *"You would get sent out of class and then we'd end up talking about all sorts of things because you'd refuse to go back to class."*

She smiled.

I was remembering the first day I met her and how I'd wanted to help her avoid In School Suspension, while still righting her wrongs. In lieu of ISS, I asked her to arrive early the following day to help the custodian, who was tremendously cool. She amicably obliged. It seemed like a perfect solution. *You took from us, now you can help us.*

The following morning, she armed herself in plastic gloves and went out to the field to pick up our student body's trash and place it in the bucket we'd provided. I recall feeling triumphant, thinking I'd "punished" her while still helping the school and not having her miss any additional class time.

My feeling of glee was cut short before lunch, when she was brought back into the office because it was reported that she was seen in the bathroom with pot. Sabine claimed that she'd found the pot on the field earlier that morning and was trying to be a good citizen by flushing it down the toilet.

Since we had no evidence, one way or another, we let her story stand and sent her back to class with her hundredth reminder about just saying "No" to drugs. My principal, who liked to give me a hard time for being a positive-minded rookie, enjoyed herself for the rest of the day, making many humorous remarks about how "well" my creative punishment had worked. *"Nice work, Wilson! Way to send her out to find pot and God knows what else on the outer grounds of our property just before school...so she can bring it back into the building."*

I smiled at that memory and at all the other memories of my restorative justice work coming back to bite me in the butt. I was brought back to reality by the sound of a sweet voice.

"Oh yeah!" Sabine said, interrupting my memories. *"You look exactly the same. Only your hair is lighter. You haven't changed a bit. Except for your hair of course."*

I laughed, not even realizing my hair was lighter. I feel like I've had the same hair since high school, but now that I have to cover a few grays (which my hair guy calls "clear hair"), perhaps it has gotten a bit lighter. I remembered that Sabine used to have lighter hair as well. It was waist-length and blonde, always brushed and styled beautifully. Everything about her was beautiful.

Then I recalled the night she wasn't so beautiful. Our principal was chaperoning the football game and texted me that she'd found Sabine intoxicated. There were meetings to follow and she would face an expulsion hearing. The result of that hearing was that she was going to stay in school and her disciplinarian dad, who lived a few towns away, was going to become more involved.

That worked for a while…till it didn't.

Teachers would say things to me like, *"Something has to be done about Sabine because what I am doing is working for everybody else."* And *"I'm done with her."*

I remember responding, *"You don't get to be done."* But I understood the sentiment.

Sometimes I too felt "done." Like the time they radioed me because she would not sit in her seat. When I went to figure out what was going on, Sabine was standing there with her beautiful long hair, in her adorable outfit, refusing to go where she was asked. The teacher had created a seating chart to solve a few problems and Sabine was absolutely not going to sit next to the person she was assigned to sit next to.

"Sabine, why can't you just suck it up and deal with it like everybody else?" I pleaded with her.

She refused repeatedly and adamantly, so we took our conversation out into the privacy of the hallway, which was empty between classes. Sabine explained the situation with the student and her angst about it all. I nodded in understanding, but still held no sympathy. *"Thank you for explaining. But this isn't Burger King. You don't get to have it your way. Sometimes, we just have to roll with the punches."*

She asked if she could go to ISS instead of class. I told her she could come to my office for the remainder of this class, write a reflection about the situation to give to her teacher after class, then go on with her day.

She complied and we got talking about the art on my wall and how she wanted to work in a quaint setting with lots of art around her. She could be so pleasant and so lovely. In these moments of conversation, it was hard to fathom the other side of her nature, when she'd resist and rebel against authority whenever she disagreed with the decision or assignment or method.

The same soft voice and giant eyes, from my office all those years ago, ushered me back to the present, *"You still smell the same."* Sabine said smiling, as she handed me my soup and croissant "to go."

When I reached into my wallet for my credit card, she said, *"And I see you still wear all your same rings."*

I laughed out loud. I couldn't help being amused at the thought of all the time and input I poured into Sabine, trying to help her reflect on her behaviors, actions, and inaction. Meanwhile, she was noticing my hair color, perfume, and rings.

I thought about Maya Angelou's quote, *"People will forget what you said. People will forget what you did. But they will never forget the way you made them feel."*

I smiled at Sabine and commented in like. I told her I liked her hair dark and I liked the way she had it all tied up. I told her it was wonderful to see her. And I meant it.

She filled me in on her life: *"After you guys kicked me out, I moved in with my dad and I've been there ever since."* She concluded, *"I'm going to graduate high school soon."*

"Of course you are," I said. *"Because you are amazing and because when you set your mind to do something, you make it happen."*

I hesitated to ask, because life does not happen in a straight line. We tend to meander back and forth before we find a path worth traveling. I never want students to feel like they are on a pre-cut trajectory to go from high school straight into college, but I overcame my hesitation and inquired, *"What are your thoughts about after high school?"*

She smiled more brightly, her smile laced with irony, *"I'm going to study psychology."* She paused. *"I want to be a counselor."*

"Of course you do." I said again. And I meant it. I have no doubt that Sabine Scolinos will be a counselor if that is what she sets her mind to. As I grabbed my food to leave, I smiled because she used to call me "the trouble counselor." *"You know,"* she'd say, *"The lady we go to when we are in trouble, but she counsels us."*

I would always tell her I wasn't a counselor. But she would always tell me she didn't care. I'm not sure she even remembered my name. But she remembered my scent, my essence. As I started to walk away, I turned back, drawn by the timing of our encounter.

"Guess what Sabine?" She smiled, waiting for the rest. *"I just finished writing a book about my work with students like you."*

Her response was genuine and the best I could have hoped for, *"That's great,"* she said sincerely. And added, with a note of encouragement, *"I can't wait to read it."* I asked for her number and I told her I'd text her. She smiled her radiant, beautiful smile, and I am certain, had there not been a counter between us, we would have embraced.

I all but floated back to my gate, ready for my flight, inwardly celebrating the fact that Sabine had "made it." She was amazing at her job and she had plans for her future. She was going to be OK!

I pulled out my phone to text the principal who used to give me such a hard time about all my creative, restorative work. Even though she is no longer at that school or in our district, she is still a high school principal and I knew she would celebrate Sabine's success and near-graduation-status with me.

Her response, although positive in regards to Sabine, was dismal. That very day, another student, from our same school, a year behind Sabine, was incarcerated for attempted murder. His stunning sandy hair and blue-eyed-self had seen fit to break into a home with a deadly weapon. He fired it with an intent to kill. Thankfully, his target lived and is expected to make a full recovery.

As I sat by the window waiting for my plane to board, I felt blindsided by emotional whiplash. I wondered, *"Where does one grief end and a victory begin and where does that one victory end and another grief begin?"*

My plane boarded and as I sat pensive in my seat, I picked up the book I'd ordered from Amazon to read on this trip. I was thankful for the reprieve from writing my own book, and eager to read someone else's. Fittingly, it was *Tattoos on the Heart,* by Gregory Boyle.

He too suffered the storms and rode the wild waves of working with gangsters. He founded Homeboy Ministries in LA and documented the success stories and tragedies of his journey. The universe must have known that I would need to read his story just as I was contemplating my own.

I landed in my hometown, greeted by my life-long friends. One friend is the Executive Director for a non-profit that benefits kids like the ones I write about and serve. The other is an attorney, who is nothing if not a loyal friend. These are the girls I grew up with, who know who I am at my very core.

As I sat before them, pondering the dichotomy I'd just witnessed, from the airport encounter with Sabine to the news report on the attempted murder, I figured, whom better to confess my doubts and insecurities to?

And so, I revealed my soul to my childhood turned teenaged, turned adult friends as I'd done so many times before. They listened with patient sympathy as I questioned my intentions and described my insecurities.

I sigh, *"Now that I'm back in the classroom, trying to practice what I am preaching, I'm drained and disheartened. At least two days a week at some point in the day, I contemplate quitting or early retirement."* They sip wine and listen.

I continue, *"How can I write a book about relentless hope and still suffer from such immense insecurity and doubt?"*

My high-powered attorney friend, who represents wealthy and famous people, under enormous pressure constantly, is no stranger to doubt or to courage, which is one of the things I love most about her. Another thing that I love about her is that she always speaks the truth. Even when it hurts. Still, most endearing and impressive, is her ability to understand complex problems, while boiling her complicated, responsive advice down to a single sentence.

"You wouldn't need hope if your work did not involve despair."

Her wisdom fueled a final episode to my written saga. When I got home, I sat down to write my conclusion.

Chapter 15

Hope

(An Attempt at Concluding)

"We are all just trying to find our own personal limits.
For some, victory is the only acceptable outcome.
Others are happy just to make it onto the track.
We are all taking an extraordinary challenge…
We're all living a dream to be a better,
more interesting, more focused version of our everyday selves.
The pursuit of that dream gives structure to our lives."

- John Bingham

A few decades ago, I was a high school student. It's funny how we all take high school for granted. But if we really stop to think about it, the concept of high school is remarkable. Truly.

First of all, it is remarkable because in my mom's lifetime, not all kids got to go to high school; they were needed on the farm. For others, it was a segregated experience. And I don't mean segregated in terms of cliques,

I mean segregated by race. When my mother was in high school, a vast amount of people still believed that separate was equal.

Through the decades, we merged all the people. And merging people is messy work. Our law makers said that everyone was entitled to a free education. Everyone. If you are homeless, you still get two free meals a day and a chance to learn. If your parents are migrant workers, you can still learn alongside of your parents' bosses. That is kind of crazy if you stop to think about it. And not only are we educating everyone and merging everyone, but we keep cutting the budget at the same time we are demanding more rigor and higher test scores.

I imagine education to be a giant field and everyone gets to play. Except some people can afford cleats and uniforms and private coaching and others just show up in whatever they have and do whatever they can. Some kids don't even know what game we are playing, let alone how to play it and they are not sure they trust the referees to keep things fair. That is public education.

Someday, (and I hope it is a day is in my own lifetime), all of our kids can be properly clothed and convinced of their important role on our team. They will all trust the fairness of the game and those who determine the penalties. But this is not what I see on a regular basis. I mourn this reality every single day when I go to work.

As much as I mourn the reality, I also believe, perhaps recklessly, perhaps righteously, perhaps relentlessly, that what I do can make a positive difference in the field we all play and practice on. Recently, I had to put this belief into words because I was unexpectedly involved in a very serious conversation about education.

A good friend of mine is a middle school teacher and he was on the ledge. Not a real ledge, with a giant drop, but the kind of ledge that makes you question everything you do and why you do it. He has been teaching adolescents for over twenty years. No small feat. He is the kind of guy you'd want your own child to have for a middle school teacher. He's also the guy you'd want at your party because he makes you laugh, without trying to be the star of the show and without trying to steal anyone's thunder.

My friend is humble and kind and can easily admit to things he does not know. He is also the kind of guy who will ask questions to learn more. But no matter what, at some point in a conversation with him, you are bound to have a laugh-out-loud moment, because he is funny and he believes that humor can build bridges and bring joy.

Our current conversation was about his work challenges. He took on a somber tone. There were no typical funny remarks or laugh-out-loud moments. He was discouraged as he dismally described his work obstacles and the climate of his setting.

"It seems to get harder every year. Everyone wants data. They want to push the numbers around and line them up and make sense of them. They add kids to my classes and there are so many, I can't even begin to try to reach them all individually."

I nod. I sigh. This is not a new notion. Not a unique conversation. This sentiment is echoed by educators all over the state, at every educational level, K-12.

He continued, *"I remember when my old students would come back and tell me that they were going into teaching because of me. They said I helped them enjoy school. Now, no one comes back. I feel like I can't reach them."*

I nod again. I sigh again. *What can I say? What would you say?* I mean, maybe he has lost that loving feeling because he got older or more cynical. But this guy isn't like that. He is still youthful and vibrant. He's not the pull-the-old-file-out and re-teach-old-stuff kind of guy.

"That sucks," I say. Because there is a long pause and because I don't know what else to say. It makes me sad to see my funny friend discouraged. It makes me heartbroken to see another dedicated educator burning out because hope gets buried beneath our obligations, agendas and spreadsheets.

And then, I started thinking about this book and about the stories of all the students, about my own story. I thought about how difficult it is to be a student nowadays. After all, we know it's hard to be a teacher, but at least we get paid. *What about our students? Especially the ones that school is hard for? Especially the ones that don't have cleats or uniforms, who don't know how to play the game? Especially the ones who don't trust the referees? Can they trust their teachers?*

As I let my mind wander off to stare at the Christmas decorations, still up in January, I thought about how much I hated middle school when I was a student and that made me think about all the kids I know who also hate middle school. As I sat there, side by side with my funny friend, I pictured what it might be like to be in his class.

"Um Ehren?"

"Yeah." He too was staring at the dangling decorations, perhaps dreading the process of taking them down, dreading the fact that tomorrow would begin another work week, wondering how he would get everything done and where he would find the energy to power through.

"About your teaching," I cleared my throat, knowing a ramble was soon to follow. *"I bet you are the highlight of your kids' day. I mean, picture their lives. Middle school is hard. Their locker jams, kids say mean things, they don't get along with their parents, and they come into your*

c. iss and you tell them the stories of the past. You teach them history. You make them laugh. I bet you are the brightest spot in their day."

My funny friend teared up.

Like me, he is so overwhelmed with the work load and obligations set upon him by law makers, tax payers, board members, and all the stake-holders of this grand profession that he forgot the very heartbeat of his work, his students.

He looked away and though I could not see his eyes, I saw his heart. It was a heart that never stopped beating for his students. He hoped to do more for them and be more for them, but he was simply overpowered and undernourished. This profession will do that to a person. It will hide your hope in a hard to reach spot.

"Ehren."

"Yeah," he said, wiping at his eyes.

"Tomorrow, tell your kids a funny story. Make them laugh. Be the best moment of their day. Then remember your work is hard, but it is not in vain. Do what you love. Do what matters. Who knows your kids and what they need better than you? What are all the stake-holders going to do? Fire a passionate, well-meaning, experienced teacher because he took his eyes off the data and put them back on the students?"

He smiled and told me a funny story about a teacher in his district who almost did get fired and we both laughed out loud. And laughing with him reminded me of how important laughing is. And hearing him tell me more stories about students he's spent extra time with reminded me of a teacher who did something unforgettable for me.

When I was in high school, I had one particular teacher who was not very flashy or engaging. One might have called him simply, mediocre. I mean, he was polite and he came prepared and we did work, but, I don't remember anything I learned or did in his class. I think it was freshman level history or something like that.

I'm not saying he was a bad teacher. I'm saying I was a bad student. I didn't care about much beyond the sport I was playing in that particular season. I worked hard enough in school to keep my parents from bugging me and to stay on the team. That's about it. I did not care about life-long learning or about being "college and career ready," I cared only about the next game and the upcoming practice that would help me do well in the next game. Sports got me through classes.

One day, as I plodded through the routines of a 15-year-old who didn't care about life-long learning, my locker jammed, or I dropped my books, or some other miserable thing happened to cause me to run late. *Stupid school,* I thought as I slammed my locker shut and rushed off.

Most teachers were cool if you came in a few seconds after the bell. If you appeared to have hurried or attempted to be there on time, most would let it slide. Unfortunately for me at that moment, this was not the case. My math teacher, Mr. Cashmere, let nothing slide, especially for me. He was a cross country coach and a very precise, disciplined man. He felt that punctuality was paramount and that athletes should be role models. I know this because he had already marked me tardy twice. Each time, I had arrived mere seconds after the bell.

This would be my third tardy. Third tardy meant detention. Detention meant missing after school sports practice. Missing the practice before the game meant I could not start in the game.

All this sent me into panic mode and I hustled. I rushed. I hurried. As I made my mad dash across campus to class, the tardy bell rang.

I slowed to a stop, pondering what to do. *Do I go to the office and try to explain and hope they give me a pass? Do I just walk in late and hope this one time he lets it slide? Do I just forget about it, stop caring and miss practice, then get yelled at by my coach, and sit out the start of our next game?*

This dilemma does not matter one shred to my adult self. I cringe sheepishly when I consider all the problems in the world at that time and that somehow this little tardy felt more urgent than all of the troubles that plagued the rest of the planet. But my 15 year-old-self is not my adult self and things were rough at home. Sports was my sanctuary, my escape, my chance to enjoy a small slice of my miserable adolescence.

With my head down, I inched my way to class, preparing myself to endure the inevitable. I walked slowly, watching each foot fall on the uneven blacktop, heavy math textbook in hand, defeated, I staggered. My face must have revealed my disappointment because I heard a concerned voice call my name.

"Christy?"

I looked up. *Great,* I thought as I rolled my eyes. It was my old history teacher, Mr. Newkirk. The one whose class I sat in everyday for an entire term, but for the life of me, could not remember one thing I wrote, read, created or learned.

"Christy," he said again as he hustled in my direction. *Excellent,* I thought sarcastically, as I began to feel even more sorry for myself. *Now I'm going to be late AND have to endure a separate conversation, (probably lecture) from yet another high school adult figure.*

"Hey Christy, wait up. I'll walk with you. Where are you headed?" he asked, his long legs making efficient strides as he moved in my direction.

"Um, math," I said, noting his dorky tie, so awkwardly attached to his even less-stylish shirt. For an instant, I actually felt sorry for him and for all our male teachers for that matter, forced to wear dorky ties because

they either didn't care enough about fashion or didn't make enough money to afford better ones. Mr. Newkirk had clearly been a ball player and was built to wear athletic attire, not dated ties.

He nodded sympathetically. *"Who's your math teacher?"* His wispy, blond hair shifted across his face.

"Mr. Cashmere," I mumbled, dreading what lay ahead.

He brushed his hair to the side and casually asked about my older brother and how he was doing in college. He had coached him and remembered how our whole family faithfully attended each game.

"He's good. He's thinking about red-shirting this year so he can practice with the team." For the briefest of moments, I had a warm spot in my heart, thinking about my brother, missing him, hoping he was happier at college than I was here in my miserable high school existence.

As we approached Mr. Cashmere's classroom, my thoughts chilled. They turned to dread when Mr. Newkirk casually asked, *"When's your next game?"*

"Tomorrow," I mumbled regretfully as we stood by the door. This tardy meant I'd be spending the first part of that game on the bench.

Mr. Newkirk kindly opened the door for me and waved at Mr. Cashmere, who had already begun. I slid shamefully into my seat and opened my math book. That's when it happened.

I heard Mr. Newkirk's voice, *"I'm sorry she was late. She was with me."*

I froze. Stunned. *Did he really just say that?* I wasn't "with" him. I was late. I was alone. *He came to be with me.*

In that moment, I realized I adored Mr. Newkirk. Not because he was a gifted teacher, or because he was a handsome jock in a dorky tie, but because he was kind.

His kindness made me want to be kind. I'm positive that after that I vowed to try harder in my classes, or at least smile more, or not complain as much to my friends about school.

Truthfully, I doubt that I actually did any of that, but what I am sure of is this: I never forgot Ed Newkirk or his generous gesture. I forgot every other thing he taught or did, but I remember that day, that moment when he was *with me.*

Throughout the rest of my high school years, I would wave across campus to him. Every now and then we would find ourselves on the same path and we'd exchange pleasantries. I never thought about his ties or his hair or his long strides. I only thought about the fact that he was *with me.*

Ed Newkirk had no idea that he saved me from detention or from not starting in a game. He didn't know that my home life was a wreck or that I hated almost every minute of high school. He just saw a student walking alone and decided to walk with her. It was awkward, but it was also gracious.

Mr. Newkirk didn't know I would grow up to be a teacher. He did not know I would later be the person students who got in trouble were sent to. He could not have known his lasting impact, nor how many students I have walked to class in the course of my career. And I always open the door and say, *"Sorry s/he's late. S/he was with me."*

Do our kids know that we are with them? Does my funny friend, Ehren, even realize that by telling stories and making his kids laugh, he is showing them he is *with* them? When the bell rings and he welcomes them at his door, does he realize he could well be the best part of their middle school day? I bet every person reading this has had the chance to be an Ed Newkirk or an Ehren to some unfortunate, forlorn kid. If not, your time will come.

After all, we educators are door openers. We hold the door with one hand and hope in the other, like a butterfly ready to take flight.

Afterword

When I told a friend that I wanted to write about a few of my students, he loaned me his copy of *Bird by Bird* by Anne Lamott. Lamott's candid observations caused me to consider the work we do as a bold act that leads to shared beauty.

"When people shine a light on their monster, we find out how similar most of our monsters are."

I welcome the notion that I'm not as different from my homeless and gangster kids as I am similar. We are all overcoming fears and obstacles and trying to move forward in this wide world.

"Your anger and damage and grief are the way to the truth."

I met a few students who came loaded with grief and scarred with damage. I think I failed some of them. But they taught me priceless lessons that helped me avoid failing others. They taught me that we have more in common than we think.

What are the stories behind our students? Teachers should be given a headlamp and a shovel along with their badge and key because we do a lot of digging. We dig to learn about ourselves, our students, and the world we live in. The light exposes our findings, as shameful as they are lovely, as devastating as they are precious. What we find connects us to the lives we teach. Our own fears and shame and ego and demons and devastations are not so different from those of our students.

If I am to find their treasures, I must face and accept their truths. When I listen, they offer their golden gifts, earned and brought at a cost. Pride may have been at stake. Risk of failure was eminent. *What if I rejected their gift or deemed their truth unworthy?*

Still, they found the courage to share. And their truth connects to my own. A teacher, whose best intentions are ever-interrupted by the complexities of young lives, difficult lessons, and an insecure, unpredictable, and pain-filled world. Their courage gives me strength as I stand and deliver.

Acknowledgments

I always enjoy reading other people's acknowledgements because our grandest projects are never completed in isolation. We are inspired by others, corrected, rejected, and affirmed by the lives we encounter and the conversations we have.

It would be impossible for me to recognize everyone who has shaped this book. I would need to catalog every student, colleague and boss I've ever had. Every person I sat next to on an airplane or bus or bar stool, every neighbor, every friend, every protagonist and antagonist in education, every conversation, every debate, for it has all shaped and sharpened my thinking and my writing. My story is one of collective influence.

Even still, certain lives rise to the surface as main characters in my setting. My husband, Dan, a man of few words, yet wise in thought, has listened to thousands of rants and questions. He does not work in the educational field, but throughout our years and seasons of life together, he's provided clarity of thought and the encouragement I've needed to rise in the face of fear. He has heard me brag as well as cry when I recount interactions with students and teachers. He nods and listens. When I am wise enough to do the same, his responses contribute to both my sanity and my progress.

My daughter, Sydney, always reminds me that life can be lived largely, which also means we may fall hard. She shows me that scrapes and bruises, though always a part of the journey, hardly diminish the joys. She reminds me to be the kind of teacher I want my own child to have. She offers a student's perspective to all of my teacher woes and reminds me that empathy is paramount. She walks, runs, and plays with me; and because of my experiences with her, my life is richer and my writing is more well-rounded.

My own mother, Dee Engel, impacted my world view profoundly. She taught me to look for the strengths in others. She lived her life as a humble leader, who knew her successes were linked to the lives she led. She valued custodians as much as supervisors and sent them all birthday cards. She made a career of helping those around her spread their wings. Her modeling has served me well. When people feel valued, they work harder for you. That notion was woven into the pages of this book.

Ode to friends and family members who read every word of this book, before it was refined and smoothed over. Katy Abraham (who read three different drafts, for the price of none), thank you for your honesty and writing advice on the trails of Forest Park and in the booth of our McMenamin's pub.

Thank you, Amy Stringer and Kristin Guelsdorf, my long-time colleagues and friends, for listening to so many of these stories in person, for encouraging me to write them down, and for reading them and weighing in with complimentary thoughts and helpful critique.

To my long-time friend and college roommate, Karen Turner, who was with me at the rainy street fair when I re-encountered José and who was with me all the years before that. Thank you for fueling me with kindness and for reminding me that kids deserve the same.

To my life-long friends, Amy Duncan and Nancy Stiles, who knew me as a young student, long before I was ever a young teacher. Thank you for sipping wine with me, for helping me celebrate the completion of a daunting project, and for reminding me (in my most insecure moments) that I am not a fraud.

I'm appreciative of colleagues like Kerry Forsell, who share passion for the betterment of educators, students, and the business of education. Thank you for being a tremendous colleague and inspiring friend. You helped me stay focused on the mission of serving students, even when I was overwhelmed with the writing of this book and feeling like a complete hypocrite. As we'd power walk through hilly suburbs, you'd remind me that our labors in education are never in vain and they always serve a greater purpose.

Thank you, Tracy Wren and Chris Jacobson for volunteering to read an early draft of this book. Your encouragement fueled its completion. It was tremendously helpful to have the input of people who are not in the field, but who care very much about what happens to kids in school. Thank you for being supportive community members. We need all the support we can get!

Heidi and Paul Colligan, I'm indebted to you. I'm pretty sure that without you, this book would still just be a document on my computer. You urged it to come to life and you helped that happen. Thank you for reading an early draft and for connecting me to an editor. I'm grateful for the advice and direction you offered and I'm lucky to call you friends.

What is a writer without an editor? I will tell you. She is someone who types random thoughts that make sense only in her own mind. Then along comes a Mick Silva who asks clutch questions at key times and provides "signage" to help me travel toward my intended destination without getting lost.

Even a teacher struggles with the rules of grammar. After reading, rereading, and proofreading this book dozens of times, multiple errors were found and fixed by my friend and colleague, Cristina Tomkins. Cris, who is a mother of two and a behavioral specialist at my site, volunteered to use her amazing skill sets to copyedit this book. Thank you Cris for this tremendous labor of love.

Dear Betty Flad, you have been a supportive mentor for me. You believed in me as an educational leader, even when I was losing hope by the minute. You reminded me to search my soul to find the best in myself and the best in others. You were also kind enough to encourage me as a writer and generous enough to give your time to read and comment on this book.

To Dawn Montgomery, Sue Brent, Kevin Bacon and all the administrators in our Courage to Lead classes, our countless conversations in the gorge and those that followed affected me and inspired me. You told me to write my stories and to hurry up and finish this book. Paving a way of potential and possibility is a profound gift to give an eager learner. I hope to do for my students what you have done for me.

My mother in law, Raye Wilson, was my first reader and has been a huge support through this entire process. She believed in my ability to impact lives before I ever began writing this book. She has been an ever-encouraging force and a continual enrichment to my life.

Thank you, "sister" Sara Hunter for our many runs through 8,000+ feet altitude as we discussed the students behind these stories. I'd listen to your feedback while panting for air on the ranch roads of Colorado. You cared about these kids, without even meeting them. This made me want to write down their stories and the lessons I learned from them so others could love them too.

A teacher's delight is to see the fruit of her labor. And I am so appreciative of past students who have hunted me down and who have emailed me or come back to visit me. Thank you, Sandy Silva, for your on-going communication and for the kind words you've offered about my impact on your life. You looked beyond a young teacher's errors and short-comings and saw her efforts and her heart. You are a wise and brave person and I'm so glad that, after decades of living thousands of miles away, we are back in touch, still sharing our lives with one another. Thank you for forgiving my foibles and for allowing me to write about you.

To Dale and Julie Case, Nora Acosta, and Dulce Nash, you saw me in my lowest moments, and stood in the trenches with me as I struggled to rise and continue the course. Your pay checks were not nearly what you deserved, but you humbly gave of yourselves. I was watching and learning from you.

Thank you, Rob and Tonya Hess, Claudia Ruf, Matt Pedersen, Erica Marson, Sho Shigeoka, Jan Martin, and Erin Miles. You gave me tremendous opportunities to share my passion for students in unique and powerful ways. One of my bosses jokingly called me "unbossable." That makes some of you extra long-suffering. You all hold positions in educational leadership that are daunting. I admire your commitment to serve your staff, your teachers, and your students. Thank you for encouraging me to "go crazy" with Restorative Justice. We all deserve to be restored and we all deserve justice. Still, it is always so complicated and you supported me in my struggles, made me laugh, and reminded me the cause is worthy.

Thank you to every student in this book, whose names I altered to protect anonymity. You represent countless other priceless and treasured young lives. You bring purpose to our labors. In certain moments, you drive us a tiny bit crazy, but without you we'd be unemployed.

There are more, so many more friends, colleagues, special acquaintances and my heart swells with gratitude. I'm sorry I cannot name you all, but rest assured, your impact lives on.

56100992R00120

Made in the USA
Columbia, SC
21 April 2019